MERCURY READER

a custom publication

Communications Department
Southwestern Michigan College
For English 104
Freshman English III

Pearson Custom Publishing

New York   Boston   San Francisco
London   Toronto   Sydney   Tokyo   Singapore   Madrid
Mexico City   Munich   Paris   Cape Town   Hong Kong   Montreal

Senior Vice President, Editorial and Marketing: Patrick F. Boles
Senior Sponsoring Editor: Natalie Danner
Development Editors: Mary Kate Paris and Katherine R. Gehan
Editorial Assistant: Jill Johnson
Operations Manager: Eric M. Kenney
Database Product Manager: Jennifer Berry
Rights Manager: Katie Huha
Art Director: Renée Sartell
Cover Designers: Renée Sartell and Sharon Treacy

Cover Art: "Gigantia Mountains & Sea of Cortes," by R.G.K. Photography, Copyright © Tony Stone Images; "Dime," courtesy of the Shaw Collection.

Printed in the United States of America.

Please visit our websites at *www.pearsoncustom.com* and *www.mercuryreader.com*.

Attention bookstores: For permission to return any unsold stock, contact us at *pe-uscustomreturns@pearson.com*.

**Pearson
Custom Publishing**
is a division of

www.pearsonhighered.com

ISBN 10: 0-558-28232-6
ISBN 13: 978-0-558-28232-5

Contents

Portfolio Checklist
English 104
Southwestern Michigan College

Instructions:

1. During the course of the semester you will be given a number of writing assignments. Keep everything you do.

2. You will submit the following pieces of your work in an online folder located on your class Moodle page. See your instructor for further details.

   A. Meta Writing (This is a one or two page self-evaluation written after the work for the semester is done. Use it to introduce your work, explain its strengths and weaknesses, or describe the process which you went through when writing this semester).

   B. An in-class essay (written during class and assigned by your instructor)

   C. One polished essay (with draft work)

   D. A second polished essay (without draft work)

   E. One research paper

3. Please note the following:

   A. Your class grade will be based on all your work. Just because it doesn't make it to your portfolio doesn't mean it isn't important.

   B. The portfolios are kept in the English department as long as space allows. **Please make copies of work you would like to keep for yourself.**

   C. **You must achieve a "C-" or above on all portfolio items in order to pass the class.**

   D. Failure to submit a complete portfolio will result in an "I" or "F" grade.

Southwestern Michigan College
English Portfolio FAQ

What is a portfolio?

The English Portfolio at SMC is a collection of representative samples of your work produced during the semester and submitted by you at semester's end.

Why do I have to do it?

The portfolio process provides you the opportunity to show your best work and provides the college with a means of verifying that its standards are met by all students.

Can I choose what goes in the portfolio?

SMC requires you to include certain numbers and types of essays in your portfolio in order to provide consistency in portfolio submissions . As long as those requirements are met, you (in consultation with your instructor) may choose whichever papers you feel best represent your abilities.

When do I turn in the portfolio?

The completed portfolio will be due toward the semester's end. Your instructor   will tell you the exact date the portfolio is due.

What happens to it?

After you turn in your portfolio and it is submitted to the department by your instructor it is kept on SMC servers. It will remain there as long as there is space for it. From time to time, other instructors and outside agencies will review sample portfolios to assess the writing standards at SMC. Your name will never be used in any data that results from such assessments.

Do I get my papers back?

No. Please make copies of all work you would like to keep **before** turning in your portfolio.

What happens if I don't turn in a portfolio?

Because the portfolio represents your best work in the class and its construction is the culminating activity of the class, it is very important. Depending on your circumstances, you will receive either an "I" or an "F" for not turning in your portfolio.

Why do I have to pass everything in the portfolio?

It is in your best interests that the college maintains high standards. Passing everything in the portfolio proves that you have learned to do what the course objectives say you will learn to do.

Why should I write essays that don't make it to the portfolio?

One reason is that you will then have something to choose from when making your selections. Another reason is that the portfolio represents the **minimum** class standards. You will need to experience other types of writing assignments and write much more than is shown in the portfolio in order to make progress in your writing abilities. Remember also that your class grade is determined by the formula found in your syllabus. **Passing the portfolio is an additional requirement, not the only requirement for passing the course.**

Portfolio Evaluation Sheet

Portfolio #_____

Focus:

    1. Has a clear thesis or forecasting statement   _____

    2. Has an understandable but general thesis   _____

    3. Has a vague unifying idea but no thesis   _____

    4. Has no consistent main idea   _____

Support:

    1. Develops the topic fully, logically, and engagingly_____

    2. Develops the topic fully   _____

    3. Only vague or general support   _____

    4. Underdeveloped or irrelevant support   _____

Organization:

    1. Is organized logically, smoothly, and effectively _____

    2. Is organized with some transitions   _____

    3. Recognizable structure, but transitions are abrupt_____

    4. Very little recognizable structure   _____

Surface Errors

    1. No errors in mechanics and style   _____

    2. Very few errors in mechanics and style   _____

    3. Noticeable errors, but none too distracting   _____

    4. Difficult to read because of errors   _____

Documentation

    1. Uses MLA or APA style skillfully   _____

    2. Uses MLA or APA style mechanically   _____

    3. Inconsistent or incomplete MLA or APA style   _____

    4. Little understanding of MLA or APA style   _____

OVERALL IMPRESSION

_____High Pass   _____Pass   _____Borderline   _____Fail

The Lone Ranger and Tonto Fistfight in Heaven

Sherman Alexie

Sherman Alexie (1966–) was born on a Spokane Indian Reservation in Wellprint, Washington. His mother was Spokane while his father Coeur d'Alene. Though his life began with medical difficulties, he learned to read at three and became a star high school athlete. He graduated from Washington State University-Pullman in American Studies. In addition to writing, he has participated in the Museum of Tolerance project; appeared on the Lehrer News Hour (with President Clinton); recorded albums; performed as a standup comedian; and written and produced a film. He was awarded a Washington State Arts Commission Poetry Fellowship in 1991, and the National Endowment for the Arts Poetry Fellowship in 1992. Other awards include the PEN/Hemingway Award, the Lila Wallace Reader's Digest Writers' Award, the Before Columbus Foundation's American Book Award, and The Filmmaker's Trophy. His works include The Lone Ranger and Tonto Fistfight in Heaven *(1994),* Reservation Blues *(1996), and* The First Indian on the Moon *(2004). In this short story, a young man from the Spokane Indian Reservation travels to Seattle to fulfill his promise but, disaffected, returns back home.*

1   Too hot to sleep so I walked down to the Third Avenue 7–11 for a Creamsicle and the company of a graveyard-shift cashier. I know that game. I worked graveyard for a Seattle 7–11 and got robbed once too often. The last time the bastard locked me in the cooler. He even took my money and basketball shoes.

The graveyard-shift worker in the Third Avenue 7–11 looked like they all do. Acne scars and a bad haircut, work pants that showed off his white socks, and those cheap black shoes that have no support. My arches still ache from my year at the Seattle 7–11.

"Hello," he asked when I walked into his store. "How you doing?"

I gave him a half-wave as I headed back to the freezer. He looked me over so he could describe me to the police later. I knew the look. One of my old girlfriends said I started to look at her that way, too. She left me not long after that. No, I left her and don't blame her for anything. That's how it happened. When one person starts to look at another like a criminal, then the love is over. It's logical.

5 "I don't trust you," she said to me. "You get too angry." 5

She was white and I lived with her in Seattle. Some nights we fought so bad that I would just get in my car and drive all night, only stop to fill up on gas. In fact, I worked the graveyard shift to spend as much time away from her as possible. But I learned all about Seattle that way, driving its back ways and dirty alleys.

Sometimes, though, I would forget where I was and get lost. I'd drive for hours, searching for something familiar. Seems like I'd spent my whole life that way, looking for anything I recognized. Once, I ended up in a nice residential neighborhood and somebody must have been worried because the police showed up and pulled me over.

"What are you doing out here?" the police officer asked me as he looked over my license and registration.

"I'm lost."

10 "Well, where are you supposed to be?" he asked me, and I knew 10 there were plenty of places I wanted to be, but none where I was supposed to be.

"I got in a fight with my girlfriend," I said. "I was just driving around, blowing off steam, you know?"

"Well, you should be more careful where you drive," the officer said. "You're making people nervous. You don't fit the profile of the neighborhood."

I wanted to tell him that I didn't really fit the profile of the country but I knew it would just get me into trouble.

"Can I help you?" the 7–11 clerk asked me loudly, searching for some response that would reassure him that I wasn't an armed robber.

He knew this dark skin and long, black hair of mine was dangerous. I had potential.

15   "Just getting a Creamsicle," I said after a long interval. It was a   15
sick twist to pull on the guy, but it was late and I was bored. I grabbed my Creamsicle and walked back to the counter slowly, scanned the aisles for effect. I wanted to whistle low and menacingly but I never learned to whistle.

"Pretty hot out tonight?" he asked, that old rhetorical weather bullshit question designed to put us both at ease.

"Hot enough to make you go crazy," I said and smiled. He swallowed hard like a white man does in those situations. I looked him over. Same old green, red, and white 7–11 jacket and thick glasses. But he wasn't ugly, just misplaced and marked by loneliness. If he wasn't working there that night, he'd be at home alone, flipping through channels and wishing he could afford HBO or Showtime.

"Will this be all?" he asked me, in that company effort to make me do some impulse shopping. Like adding a clause onto a treaty. *We'll take Washington and Oregon and you get six pine trees and a brand-new Chrysler Cordoba.* I knew how to make and break promises.

"No," I said and paused. "Give me a Cherry Slushie, too."

20   "What size?" he asked, relieved.   20

"Large," I said, and he turned his back to me to make the drink. He realized his mistake but it was too late. He stiffened, ready for the gunshot or the blow behind the ear. When it didn't come, he turned back to me.

"I'm sorry," he said. "What size did you say?"

"Small," I said and changed the story.

"But I thought you said large."

25   "If you knew I wanted a large, then why did you ask me again?"   25
I asked him and laughed. He looked at me, couldn't decide if I was giving him serious shit or just goofing. There was something about him I liked, even if it was three in the morning and he was white.

"Hey," I said. "Forget the Slushie. What I want to know is if you know all the words to the theme from 'The Brady Bunch'?"

He looked at me, confused at first, then laughed.

"Shit," he said. "I was hoping you weren't crazy. You were scaring me."

"Well, I'm going to get crazy if you don't know the words."

He laughed loudly then, told me to take the Creamsicle for free. He was the graveyard-shift manager and those little demonstrations of power tickled him. All seventy-five cents of it. I knew how much everything cost.

"Thanks," I said to him and walked out the door. I took my time walking home, let the heat of the night melt the Creamsicle all over my hand. At three in the morning I could act just as young as I wanted to act. There was no one around to ask me to grow up.

In Seattle, I broke lamps. She and I would argue and I'd break a lamp, just pick it up and throw it down. At first she'd buy replacement lamps, expensive and beautiful. But after a while she'd buy lamps from Goodwill or garage sales. Then she just gave up the idea entirely and we'd argue in the dark.

"You're just like your brother," she'd yell. "Drunk all the time and stupid."

"My brother don't drink that much."

She and I never tried to hurt each other physically. I did love her, after all, and she loved me. But those arguments were just as damaging as a fist. Words can be like that, you know? Whenever I get into arguments now, I remember her and I also remember Muhammad Ali. He knew the power of his fists but, more importantly, he knew the power of his words, too. Even though he only had an IQ of 80 or so, Ali was a genius. And she was a genius, too. She knew exactly what to say to cause me the most pain.

But don't get me wrong. I walked through that relationship with an executioner's hood. Or more appropriately, with war paint and sharp arrows. She was a kindergarten teacher and I continually insulted her for that.

"Hey, schoolmarm," I asked. "Did your kids teach you anything new today?"

And I always had crazy dreams. I always have had them, but it seemed they became nightmares more often in Seattle.

In one dream, she was a missionary's wife and I was a minor war chief. We fell in love and tried to keep it secret. But the missionary caught us fucking in the barn and shot me. As I lay dying, my tribe learned of the shooting and attacked the whites all across the reservation. I died and my soul drifted above the reservation.

40 Disembodied, I could see everything that was happening. Whites 40
killing Indians and Indians killing whites. At first it was small, just
my tribe and the few whites who lived there. But my dream grew,
intensified. Other tribes arrived on horseback to continue the slaughter
of whites, and the United States Cavalry rode into battle.

The most vivid image of that dream stays with me. Three
mounted soldiers played polo with a dead Indian woman's head.
When I first dreamed it, I thought it was just a product of my anger
and imagination. But since then, I've read similar accounts of that
kind of evil in the old West. Even more terrifying, though, is the fact
that those kinds of brutal things are happening today in places like El
Salvador.

All I know for sure, though, is that I woke from that dream in
terror, packed up all my possessions, and left Seattle in the middle of
the night.

"I love you," she said as I left her. "And don't ever come back."

I drove through the night, over the Cascades, down into the
plains of central Washington, and back home to the Spokane Indian
Reservation.

45 When I finished the Creamsicle that the 7–11 clerk gave me, 45
I held the wooden stick up into the air and shouted out very loudly.
A couple lights flashed on in windows and a police car cruised by
me a few minutes later. I waved to the men in blue and they waved
back accidentally. When I got home it was still too hot to sleep so I
picked up a week-old newspaper from the floor and read.

There was another civil war, another terrorist bomb exploded,
and one more plane crashed and all aboard were presumed dead. The
crime rate was rising in every city with populations larger than
100,000, and a farmer in Iowa shot his banker after foreclosure on his
1,000 acres.

A kid from Spokane won the local spelling bee by spelling the
word *rhinoceros.*

When I got back to the reservation, my family wasn't surprised to
see me. They'd been expecting me back since the day I left for Seattle.
There's an old Indian poet who said that Indians can reside in the city,
but they can never live there. That's as close to truth as any of us can get.

Mostly I watched television. For weeks I flipped through channels, searched for answers in the game shows and soap operas. My mother would circle the want ads in red and hand the paper to me.

50   "What are you going to do with the rest of your life?" she asked.   50

"Don't know," I said, and normally, for almost any other Indian in the country, that would have been a perfectly fine answer. But I was special, a former college student, a smart kid. I was one of those Indians who was supposed to make it, to rise above the rest of the reservation like a fucking eagle or something. I was the new kind of warrior.

For a few months I didn't even look at the want ads my mother circled, just left the newspaper where she had set it down. After a while, though, I got tired of television and started to play basketball again. I'd been a good player in high school, nearly great, and almost played at the college I attended for a couple years. But I'd been too out of shape from drinking and sadness to ever be good again. Still, I liked the way the ball felt in my hands and the way my feet felt inside my shoes.

At first I just shot baskets by myself. It was selfish, and I also wanted to learn the game again before I played against anybody else. Since I had been good before and embarrassed fellow tribal members, I knew they would want to take revenge on me. Forget about the cowboys versus Indians business. The most intense competition on any reservation is Indians versus Indians.

But on the night I was ready to play for real, there was this white guy at the gym, playing with all the Indians.

55   "Who is that?" I asked Jimmy Seyler.   55

"He's the new BIA[1] chief's kid."

"Can he play?"

"Oh, yeah."

And he could play. He played Indian ball, fast and loose, better than all the Indians there.

60   "How long's he been playing here?" I asked.   60

"Long enough."

I stretched my muscles, and everybody watched me. All these Indians watched one of their old and dusty heroes. Even though I had played most of my ball at the white high school I went to, I was still all Indian, you know? I was Indian when it counted, and this BIA kid needed to be beaten by an Indian, any Indian.

I jumped into the game and played well for a little while. It felt good. I hit a few shots, grabbed a rebound or two, played enough defense to keep the other team honest. Then that white kid took over the game. He was too good. Later, he'd play college ball back East and would nearly make the Knicks team a couple years on. But we didn't know any of that would happen. We just knew he was better that day and every other day.

The next morning I woke up tired and hungry, so I grabbed the want ads, found a job I wanted, and drove to Spokane to get it. I've been working at the high school exchange program ever since, typing and answering phones. Sometimes I wonder if the people on the other end of the line know that I'm Indian and if their voices would change if they did know.

65 One day I picked up the phone and it was her, calling from Seattle.

"I got your number from your mom," she said. "I'm glad you're working."

"Yeah, nothing like a regular paycheck."

"Are you drinking?"

"No, I've been on the wagon for almost a year."

70 "Good."

The connection was good. I could hear her breathing in the spaces between our words. How do you talk to the real person whose ghost has haunted you? How do you tell the difference between the two?

"Listen," I said. "I'm sorry for everything."

"Me, too."

"What's going to happen to us?" I asked her and wished I had the answer for myself.

75 "I don't know," she said. "I want to change the world."

These days, living alone in Spokane, I wish I lived closer to the river, to the falls where ghosts of salmon jump. I wish I could sleep. I put down my paper or book and turn off all the lights, lie quietly in the dark. It may take hours, even years, for me to sleep again. There's nothing surprising or disappointing in that.

I know how all my dreams end anyway.

End Notes

1. Bureau of Indian Affairs.

Dover Beach

Matthew Arnold

Matthew Arnold (1822-1888) was born outside London but spent his early life at Rugby School where his father was a headmaster. He attended Oxford and later became inspector of schools for the British government. His two volumes of poetry, Poems: A New Edition *(1853-4) and* New Poems *(1867), made his reputation as a poet. In 1857 he was appointed professor of poetry at Oxford, where he published* Essays on Criticism *(1865, 1888) and* Culture and Anarchy *(1869). Later in life Arnold made his mark as a theologian with* Literature and Dogma *(1872) and* Last Essay on Church and Religion *(1877). "Dover Beach" was published in his second collection of poems in 1867.*

1   The sea is calm to-night.
The tide is full, the moon lies fair
Upon the straits;—on the French coast the light
Gleams and is gone; the cliffs of England stand,
5   Glimmering and vast, out in the tranquil bay.
Come to the window, sweet is the night-air!

Only, from the long line of spray
Where the sea meets the moon-blanch'd land,
Listen! you hear the grating roar
10   Of pebbles which the waves draw back, and fling,
At their return, up the high strand,
Begin, and cease, and then again begin,
With tremulous cadence slow, and bring
The eternal note of sadness in.

15 Sophocles long ago
Heard it on the Aegean, and it brought
Into his mind the turbid ebb and flow
Of human misery; we
Find also in the sound a thought,
20 Hearing it by this distant northern sea.

The Sea of Faith
Was once, too, at the full, and round earth's shore
Lay like the folds of a bright girdle furl'd.
But now I only hear
25 Its melancholy, long, withdrawing roar,
Retreating, to the breath
Of the night-wind, down the vast edges drear
And naked shingles of the world.

Ah, love, let us be true
30 To one another! for the world, which seems
To lie before us like a land of dreams,
So various, so beautiful, so new,
Hath really neither joy, nor love, nor light,
Nor certitude, nor peace, nor help for pain;
35 And we are here as on a darkling plain
Swept with confused alarms of struggle and flight,
Where ignorant armies clash by night.

The Lesson

Toni Cade Bambara

Toni Cade Bambara (1939–1995) was born in New York City and attended Queens College, the University of Florence, the City University of New York, and the New School for Social Research, as well as dance studios and other institutes. Her professional life was as varied as her education, including social work and teaching in women's studies and literature programs. She wrote much fiction and many essays for a wide range of magazines as well as several books. Her short stories are collected into three books: Gorilla, My Love *(1972),* The Sea Birds Are Still Alive *(1977), and* The Salt Eaters *(1980). Her novel* If Blessing Comes *was published in 1987. The story "The Lesson" was printed in* Gorilla, My Love. *Like a personal essay, this story leads the reader through an experience that grows to a larger significance than the event itself may first suggest.*

1   Back in the days when everyone was old and stupid or young and foolish and me and Sugar were the only ones just right, this lady moved on our block with nappy hair and proper speech and no makeup. And quite naturally we laughed at her, laughed the way we did at the junk man who went about his business like he was some big-time president and his sorry-ass horse his secretary. And we kinda hated her too, hated the way we did the winos who cluttered up our parks and pissed on our handball walls and stank up our hallways and stairs so you couldn't halfway play hide-and-seek without a goddamn gas mask. Miss Moore was her name. The only woman on the block with no first name. And she was black as hell, cept for her feet, which were fish-white and spooky. And she was always planning these

boring-ass things for us to do, us being my cousin, mostly, who lived on the block cause we all moved North the same time and to the same apartment then spread out gradual to breathe. And our parents would yank our heads into some kinda shape and crisp up our clothes so we'd be presentable for travel with Miss Moore, who always looked like she was going to church, though she never did. Which is just one of things the grown-ups talked about when they talked behind her back like a dog. But when she came calling with some sachet she'd sewed up or some gingerbread she'd made or some book, why then they'd all be too embarrassed to turn her down and we'd get handed over all spruced up. She'd been to college and said it was only right that she should take responsibility for the young ones' education, and she not even related by marriage or blood. So they'd go for it. Specially Aunt Gretchen. She was the main gofer in the family. You got some ole dumb shit foolishness you want somebody to go for, you send for Aunt Gretchen. She been screwed into the go-along for so long, it's a blood-deep natural thing with her. Which is how she got saddled with me and Sugar and Junior in the first place while our mothers were in a la-de-da apartment up the block having a good ole time.

So this one day Miss Moore rounds us all up at the mailbox and it's puredee hot and she's knockin herself out about arithmetic. And school suppose to let up in summer I heard, but she don't never let up. And the starch in my pinafore scratching the shit outta me and I'm really hating this nappy-head bitch and her goddamn college degree. I'd much rather go to the pool or to the show where it's cool. So me and Sugar leaning on the mailbox being surly, which is a Miss Moore word. And Flyboy checking out what everybody brought for lunch. And Fat Butt already wasting his peanut-butter-and-jelly sandwich like the pig he is. And Junebug punchin on Q.T.'s arm for potato chips. And Rosie Giraffe shifting from one hip to the other waiting for somebody to step on her foot or ask her if she from Georgia so she can kick ass, preferably Mercedes'. And Miss Moore asking us do we know what money is, like we a bunch of retards. I mean real money, she say, like it's only poker chips or monopoly papers we lay on the grocer. So right away I'm tired of this and say no. And would much rather snatch Sugar and go to the Sunset and terrorize the West Indian kids and take their hair ribbons and their money too. And Miss Moore files that remark away for next week's lesson on brotherhood, I can tell. And finally I say we oughta get to the subway cause it's cooler and besides we might meet some cute boys. Sugar done swiped her mama's lipstick, so we ready.

So we heading down the street and she's boring us silly about what things cost and what our parents make and how much goes for rent and how money ain't divided up right in this country. And then she gets to the part about we all poor and live in the slums, which I don't feature. And I'm ready to speak on that, but she steps out in the street and hails two cabs just like that. Then she hustles half the crew in with her and hands me a five-dollar bill and tells me to calculate 10 percent tip for the driver. And we're off. Me and Sugar and Junebug and Flyboy hangin out the window and hollering to everybody, putting lipstick on each other cause Flyboy a faggot anyway, and making farts with our sweaty armpits. But I'm mostly trying to figure how to spend this money. But they all fascinated with the meter ticking and Junebug starts laying bets as to how much it'll read when Flyboy can't hold his breath no more. Then Sugar lays bets as to how much it'll be when we get there. So I'm stuck. Don't nobody want to go for my plan, which is to jump out at the next light and run off to the first bar-b-que we can find. Then the driver tells us to get the hell out cause we there already. And the meter reads eighty-five cents. And I'm stalling to figure out the tip and Sugar say give him a dime. And I decide he don't need it bad as I do, so later for him. But then he tries to take off with Junebug foot still in the door so we talk about his mama something ferocious. Then we check out that we on Fifth Avenue and everybody dressed up in stockings. One lady in a fur coat, hot as it is. White folks crazy.

"This is the place," Miss Moore say, presenting it to us in the voice she uses at the museum. "Let's look in the windows before we go in."

5   "Can we steal?" Sugar asks very serious like she's getting the   5
ground rules squared away before she plays. "I beg your pardon," says Miss Moore, and we fall out. So she leads us around the windows of the toy store and me and Sugar screamin, "This is mine, that's mine, I gotta have that, that was made for me, I was born for that," till Big Butt drowns us out.

"Hey, I'm goin to buy that there."

"That there? You don't even know what it is, stupid."

"I do so," he say punchin on Rosie Giraffe. "It's a microscope."

"Watcha gonna do with a microscope, fool?"

10   "Look at things."   10

"Like what, Ronald?" ask Miss Moore. And Big Butt ain't got the first notion. So here go Miss Moore gabbing about the thousands of bacteria in a drop of water and the somethin or other in a speck of blood and the million and one living things in the air around us is invisible to the naked eye. And what she say that for? Junebug go to town on that "naked" and we rolling. Then Miss Moore ask what it cost. So we all jam into the window smudgin it up and the price tag say $300. So then she ask how long'd take for Big Butt and Junebug to save up their allowances. "Too long," I say. "Yeh," adds Sugar, "outgrown it by that time." And Miss Moore say no, you never outgrow learning instruments. "Why, even medical students and interns and," blah, blah, blah. And we ready to choke Big Butt for bringing it up in the first damn place.

"This here costs four hundred eighty dollars," say Rosie Giraffe. So we pile up all over her to see what she pointin out. My eyes tell me it's a chunk of glass cracked with something heavy, and different-color inks dripped into the splits, then the whole thing put into a oven or something. But the $480 it don't make sense.

"That's a paperweight made of semi-precious stones fused together under tremendous pressure," she explains slowly, with her hands doing the mining and all the factory work.

"So what's a paperweight?" asks Rosie Giraffe.

15   "To weigh paper with, dumbbell," say Flyboy, the wise man from   15
the East.

"Not exactly," say Miss Moore, which is what she say when you warm or way off too. "It's to weigh paper down so it won't scatter and make your desk untidy." So right away me and Sugar curtsy to each other and then to Mercedes who is more the tidy type.

"We don't keep paper on top of the desk in my class," say Junebug, figuring Miss Moore crazy or lyin one.

"At home, then," she say. "Don't you have a calendar and a pencil case and a blotter and a letter-opener on your desk at home where you do your homework?" And she know damn well what our homes look like cause she nosys around in them every chance she gets.

"I don't even have a desk," say Junebug. "Do we?"

20   "No. And I don't get no homework neither," say Big Butt.   20

"And I don't even have a home," say Flyboy like he do at school to keep the white folks off his back and sorry for him. Send this poor kid to camp posters, is his specialty.

"I do," says Mercedes. "I have a box of stationery on my desk and a picture of my cat. My godmother bought the stationery and the desk. There's a big rose on each sheet and the envelopes smell like roses."

"Who wants to know about your smelly-ass stationery," say Rosie Giraffe fore I can get my two cents in.

"It's important to have a work area all your own so that . . . "

25 "Will you look at this sailboat, please," say Flyboy, cuttin her off 25 and pointin to the thing like it was his. So once again we tumble all over each other to gaze at this magnificent thing in the toy store which is just big enough to maybe sail two kittens across the pond if you strap them to the posts tight. We all start reciting the price tag like we in assembly. "Handcrafted sailboat of fiberglass at one thousand one hundred ninety-five dollars."

"Unbelievable," I hear myself say and am really stunned. I read it again for myself just in case the group recitation put me in a trance. Same thing. For some reason this pisses me off. We look at Miss Moore and she lookin at us, waiting for I dunno what.

"Who'd pay all that when you can buy a sailboat set for a quarter at Pop's, a tube of glue for a dime, and a ball of string for eight cents? It must have a motor and a whole lot else besides," I say. "My sailboat cost me about fifty cents."

"But will it take water?" say Mercedes with her smart ass.

"Took mine to Alley Pond Park once," say Flyboy. "String broke. Lost it. Pity."

30 "Sailed mine in Central Park and it keeled over and sank. Had to 30 ask my father for another dollar."

"And you got the strap," laugh Big Butt. "The jerk didn't even have a string on it. My old man wailed on his behind."

Little Q.T. was staring hard at the sailboat and you could see he wanted it bad. But he too little and somebody'd just take it from him. So what the hell. "This boat for kids, Miss Moore?"

"Parents silly to buy something like that just to get all broke up," say Rosie Giraffe.

"That much money it should last forever," I figure.

35 "My father'd buy it for me if I wanted it." 35

"Your father, my ass," say Rosie Giraffe getting a chance to finally push Mercedes.

"Must be rich people shop here," say Q.T.

"You are a very bright boy," say Flyboy. "What was your first clue?" And he rap him on the head with the back of his knuckles, since Q.T. the only one he could get away with. Though Q.T. liable to come up behind you years later and get his licks in when you half expect it.

"What I want to know," I says to Miss Moore though I never talk to her, I wouldn't give the bitch that satisfaction, "is how much a real boat costs? I figure a thousand'd get you a yacht any day."

"Why don't you check that out," she says, "and report back to the group?" Which really pains my ass. If you gonna mess up a perfectly good swim day least you could do is have some answers. "Let's go in," she say like she got something up her sleeve. Only she don't lead the way. So me and Sugar turn the corner to where the entrance is, but when we get there I kinda hang back. Not that I'm scared, what's there to be afraid of, just a toy store. But I feel funny, shame. But what I got to be shamed about? Got as much right to go in as anybody. But somehow I can't seem to get hold of the door, so I step away for Sugar to lead. But she hangs back too. And I look at her and she looks at me and this is ridiculous. I mean, damn, I have never ever been shy about doing nothing or going nowhere. But then Mercedes steps up and then Rosie Giraffe and Big Butt crowd in behind and shove, and next thing we all stuffed into the doorway with only Mercedes squeezing past us, smoothing out her jumper and walking right down the aisle. Then the rest of us tumble in like a glued-together jigsaw done all wrong. And people lookin at us. And it's like the time me and Sugar crashed into the Catholic church on a dare. But once we got in there and everything so hushed and holy and the candles and the bowin and the handkerchiefs on all the drooping heads, I just couldn't go through with the plan. Which was for me to run up to the altar and do a tap dance while Sugar played the nose flute and messed around in the holy water. And Sugar kept givin me the elbow. Then later teased me so bad I tied her up in the shower and turned it on and locked her in. And she'd be there till this day if Aunt Gretchen hadn't finally figured I was lyin about the boarder takin a shower.

Same thing in the store. We all walkin on tiptoe and hardly touchin the games and puzzles and things. And I watched Miss Moore who is steady watchin us like she waitin for a sign. Like Mama Drewery watches the sky and sniffs the air and takes note of just how much slant is in the bird formation. Then me and Sugar bump smack into each other, so busy gazing at the toys, specially the sailboat. But we don't laugh and go into our fat-lady bump-stomach routine. We just stare at that price tag. Then Sugar run a finger over the whole boat. And I'm jealous and want to hit her. Maybe not her, but I sure want to punch somebody in the mouth.

"Watcha bring us here for, Miss Moore?"

"You sound angry, Sylvia. Are you mad about something?" Givin me one of them grins like she tellin a grown-up joke that never turns out to be funny. And she's lookin very closely at me like maybe she plannin to do my portrait from memory. I'm mad, but I won't give her that satisfaction. So I slouch around the store bein very bored and say, "Let's go."

Me and Sugar at the back of the train watchin the tracks whizzin by large then small then gettin gobbled up in the dark. I'm thinkin about this tricky toy I saw in the store. A clown that somersaults on a bar then does chin-ups just cause you yank lightly at his leg. Cost $35. I could see me askin my mother for a $35 birthday clown. "You wanna who that costs what?" she'd say, cocking her head to the side to get a better view of the hole in my head. Thirty-five dollars could buy new bunk beds for Junior and Gretchen's boy. Thirty-five dollars and the whole household could visit Grandaddy Nelson in the country. Thirty-five dollars would pay for the rent and the piano bill too. Who are these people that spend that much for performing clowns and $1,000 for toy sailboats? What kinda work they do and how they live and how come we ain't in on it? Where we are is who we are, Miss Moore always pointin out. But it don't necessarily have to be that way, she always adds then waits for somebody to say that poor people have to wake up and demand their share of the pie and don't none of us know what kind of pie she talkin about in the first damn place. But she ain't so smart cause I still got her four dollars from the taxi and she ain't gettin it. Messin up my day with this shit. Sugar nudges me in my pocket and winks.

Miss Moore lines us up in front of the mailbox where we started from, seem like years ago, and I got a headache for thinkin so hard. And we lean all over each other so we can hold up under the draggy-ass lecture she always finishes us off with at the end before we thank her for borin us to tears. But she just looks at us like she readin tea leaves. Finally she say, "Well, what did you think of F.A.O. Schwarz?"

Rosie Giraffe mumbles, "White folks crazy."

"I'd like to go there again when I get my birthday money," says Mercedes, and we shove her out the pack so she has to lean on the mailbox by herself.

"I'd like a shower. Tiring day," say Flyboy.

Then Sugar surprises me by sayin, "You know, Miss Moore, I don't think all of us here put together eat in a year what that sailboat costs." And Miss Moore lights up like somebody goosed her. "And?" she say, urging Sugar on. Only I'm standin on her foot so she don't continue.

50 "Imagine for a minute what kind of society it is in which some people can spend on a toy what it would cost to feed a family of six or seven. What do you think?"

"I think," say Sugar pushing me off her feet like she never done before, cause I whip her ass in a minute, "that this is not much of a democracy if you ask me. Equal chance to pursue happiness means an equal crack at the dough, don't it?" Miss Moore is besides herself and I am disgusted with Sugar's treachery. So I stand on her foot one more time to see if she'll shove me. She shuts up, and Miss Moore looks at me, sorrowfully I'm thinkin. And somethin weird is goin on, I can feel it in my chest.

"Anybody else learn anything today?" lookin dead at me. I walk away and Sugar has to run to catch up and don't even seem to notice when I shrug her arm off my shoulder.

"Well, we got four dollars anyway," she says.

"Uh hunh."

55 "We could go to Hascombs and get half a chocolate layer and then go to the Sunset and still have plenty money for potato chips and ice-cream sodas."

"Uh hunh."

"Race you to Hascombs," she say.

We start down the block and she gets ahead which is O.K. by me cause I'm going to the West End and then over to the Drive to think this day through. She can run if she want to and even run faster. But ain't nobody gonna beat me at nuthin.

My Mother's Memoirs, My Father's Lie, and Other True Stories

Russell Banks

Russell Banks (1940–) was born in Newton, Massachusetts and was educated at Colgate University and the University of North Carolina. He has recently taught at Princeton University and Sarah Lawrence University. He began his writing career as a poet, but his reputation as a fiction writer was established with the publication of his novel, Continental Drift *(1985). Since then he has won many awards for his writing, including the American Academy and Institute of Arts and Letters Award for work of distinction in 1986, and the O. Henry Memorial Award as well as being named the official New York State author for 2004–2005. His most recent novel,* Affliction *(recently made into a movie), is set in a small town in New England, where much of his writing takes place. Previous to that work, he published* The Sweet Hereafter, *which was also made into a movie. This selection is a short story from the collection* Success Stories *(1986). In it Banks offers a powerful statement about family and the meaning of the stories they share.*

1   My mother tells me stories about her past, and I don't believe   1
them, I interpret them.

She told me she had the female lead in the Catamount High School senior play and Sonny Tufts had the male lead. She claimed that he asked her to the cast party, but by then she was in love with

---

"My Mother's Memoirs, My Father's Lie, and Other True Stories" from *Success Stories* by Russell Banks. Published by Harper & Row, 1986.

my father, a stagehand for the play, so she turned down the boy who became a famous movie actor and went to the cast party with the boy who became a New Hampshire carpenter.

She also told me that she knew the principals in Grace Metalious's novel *Peyton Place*. The same night the girl in the book murdered her father, she went afterwards to a Christmas party given by my mother and father in Catamount. "The girl acted strange," my mother said. "Kind of like she was on drugs or something, you know? And the boy she was with, one of the Goldens. He just got drunk and depressed, and then they left. The next day we heard about the police finding the girl's father in the manure pile. . . ."

"Manure pile?"

"She buried him there. And your father told me to keep quiet, not to tell a soul they were at our party on Christmas Eve. That's why our party isn't in the book or the movie they made of it," she explained.

5   She also insists, in the face of my repeated denials, that she once   5
saw me being interviewed on television by Dan Rather.

I remembered these three stories recently when, while pawing through a pile of old newspaper clippings, I came upon the obituary of Sonny Tufts. Since my adolescence, I have read two and sometimes three newspapers a day, and frequently I clip an article that for obscure or soon forgotten reasons attracts me; then I toss the clipping into a desk drawer, and every once in a while, without scheduling it, I am moved to read through the clippings and throw them out. It's an experience that fills me with a strange sadness, a kind of grief for my lost self, as if I were reading and throwing out old diaries.

But it's my mother I was speaking of. She grew up poor and beautiful in a New England mill town, Catamount, New Hampshire, the youngest of the five children of a machinist whose wife died ("choked to death on a porkchop bone"—another of her stories) when my mother was nineteen. She was invited the same year, 1933, to the Chicago World's Fair to compete in a beauty pageant but didn't accept the invitation, though she claims my father went to the fair and played his clarinet in a National Guard marching band. Her father, she said, made her stay in Catamount that summer, selling dresses for Grover Cronin's Department Store on River Street. If her mother had not died that year, she would have been able to go to the fair. "And who knows," she joked, "you might've ended up the son of Miss Chicago World's Fair of 1933."

To tell the truth, I don't know very much about my mother's life before 1940, the year I was born and started gathering material for my own stories. Like most people, I pay scant attention to the stories I'm told about lives and events that precede the remarkable event of my own birth. We all seem to tell and hear our own memoirs. It's the same with my children. I watch their adolescent eyes glaze over, their attention drift on to secret plans for the evening and weekend, as I point out the tenement on Perley Street in Catamount where I spent my childhood. Soon it will be too late, I want to say. Soon I, too, will be living in exile, retired from the cold like my mother in San Diego, alone in a drab apartment in a project by the bay, collecting social security and wondering if I'll have enough money at the end of the month for a haircut. Soon all you'll have of me will be your memories of my stories.

Everyone knows that the death of a parent is a terrible thing. But because our parents usually have not been a part of our daily lives for years, most of us do not miss them when they die. When my father died, even though I had been seeing him frequently and talking with him on the phone almost every week, I did not miss him. Yet his death was for me a terrible thing and goes on being a terrible thing now, five years later. My father, a depressed, cynical alcoholic, did not tell stories, but even if he had told stories—about his childhood in Nova Scotia, about beating out Sonny Tufts in the courtship of my mother, about playing the clarinet at the Chicago World's Fair—I would not have listened. No doubt, in his cynicism and despair of ever being loved, he knew that.

The only story my father told me that I listened to closely, visualized, and have remembered, he told me a few months before he died. It was the story of how he came to name me Earl. Naturally, as a child I asked, and he simply shrugged and said he happened to like the name. My mother corroborated the shrug. But one Sunday morning the winter before he died, three years before he planned to retire and move to a trailer down south, I was sitting across from my father in his kitchen, watching him drink tumblers of Canadian Club and ginger ale, and he wagged a finger in my face and told me that I did not know who I was named after.

"I thought no one," I said.

"When I was a kid," he said, "my parents tried to get rid of me in the summers. They used to send me to stay with my uncle Earl up on Cape Breton. He was a bachelor and kind of a hermit, and he stayed drunk most of the time. But he played the fiddle, the violin. And he loved me. He was quite a character. But then, when I was about twelve, I was old enough to spend my summers working, so they kept me down in Halifax after that. And I never saw Uncle Earl again."

He paused and sipped at his drink. He was wearing his striped pajamas and maroon bathrobe and carpet slippers and was chain-smoking Parliaments. His wife (his second—my mother divorced him when I was twelve, because of his drinking and what went with it) had gone to the market as soon as I arrived, as if afraid to leave him without someone else in the house. "He died a few years later," my father said. "Fell into a snowbank, I heard. Passed out. Froze to death."

I listened to the story and have remembered it today because I thought it was about *me*, my name, Earl. My father told it, of course, because it was about *him*, and because for an instant that cold February morning he dared to hope that his oldest son would love him.

At this moment, as I say this, I do love him, but it's too late for the saying to make either of us happy. That is why I say the death of a parent is a terrible thing.

After my father died, I asked his sister Ethel about poor old Uncle Earl. She said she never heard of the man. The unofficial family archivist and only a few years younger than my father, she surely would have known of him, would have known how my father spent his summers, would have known of the man he loved enough to name his firstborn son after.

The story simply was not true. My father had made it up.

Just as my mother's story about Sonny Tufts is not true. Yesterday, when I happened to come across the article about Sonny Tufts from the *Boston Globe,* dated June 8, 1970, and written by the late George Frazier, I wouldn't have bothered to reread it if the week before I had not been joking about Sonny Tufts with a friend, a woman who lives in Boston and whose mother died this past summer. My friend's mother's death, like my father's, was caused by acute alcoholism and had been going on for years. What most suicides accomplish in minutes, my father and my friend's mother took decades to do.

The death of my friend's mother reminded me of the consequences of the death of my father and of my mother's continuing to live. And then our chic joke about the 1940s film star ("Whatever happened to Sonny Tufts?"), a joke about our own aging, reminded me of my mother's story about the senior play in 1932, so that when I saw Frazier's obituary for Tufts, entitled "Death of a Bonesman" (Tufts had gone to Yale and been tapped for Skull and Bones), instead of tossing it back in the drawer or into the wastebasket, I read it through to the end, as if searching for a reference to my mother's having brushed him off. Instead, I learned that Bowen Charlton Tufts III, scion of an old Boston banking family, had prepped for Yale at Exeter. So that his closest connection to the daughter of a machinist in Catamount, and to me, was probably through his father's bank's ownership of the mill where the machinist ran a lathe.

I had never believed the story anyhow, but now I had proof that she made it up. Just as the fact that I have never been interviewed by Dan Rather is proof that my mother never saw me on television in her one-room apartment in San Diego being interviewed by Dan Rather. By the time she got her friend down the hall to come and see her son on TV, Dan had gone on to some depressing stuff about the Middle East.

As for Grace Metalious's characters from *Peyton Place* showing up at a Christmas party in my parents' house in Catamount, I never believed that, either. *Peyton Place* was indeed based on a true story about a young woman's murder of her father in Gilmanton, New Hampshire, a village some twenty-five miles from Catamount, but in the middle 1940s people simply did not drive twenty-five miles over snowcovered back roads on a winter night to go to a party given by strangers.

I said that to my mother. She had just finished telling me, for the hundredth time, it seemed, that someday, based on my own experiences as a child and now as an adult in New Hampshire, I should be able to write another *Peyton Place*. This was barely two months ago, and I was visiting her in San Diego, an extension of a business trip to Los Angeles, and I was seated rather uncomfortably in her one-room apartment. She is a tiny, wrenlike woman with few possessions, most of which seem miniaturized, designed to fit her small body and the close confines of her room, so that when I visit her I feel huge and oafish. I lower my voice and move with great care.

She was ironing her sheets, while I sat on the unmade sofa bed, unmade because I had just turned the mattress for her, a chore she saves for when I or my younger brother, the only large-sized people in her life now, visits her from the East. "But we *weren't* strangers to them," my mother chirped. "Your father knew the Golden boy somehow. Probably one of his local drinking friends," she said. "Anyhow, that's why your father wouldn't let me tell anyone, after the story came out in the papers, about the murder and the incest and all. . . ."

"Incest? What incest?"

"You know, the father who got killed, killed and buried in the manure pile by his own daughter because he'd been committing incest with her. Didn't you read the book?"

"No."

"Well, your father, he was afraid we'd get involved somehow. So I couldn't tell anyone about it until after the book got famous. You know, whenever I tell people out here that back in New Hampshire in the forties I knew the girl who killed her father in *Peyton Place,* they won't believe me. Well, not exactly *knew* her, but you know. . . ."

There's always someone famous in her stories, I thought. Dan Rather, Sonny Tufts, Grace Metalious (though my mother can never remember her name, only the name of the book she wrote). It's as if she hopes you will love her more easily if she is associated somehow with fame.

When you know a story isn't true, you think you don't have to listen to it. What you think you're supposed to do is interpret, as I was doing that morning in my mother's room, converting her story into a clue to her psychology, which in turn would lead me to compare it to my own psychology and, with relief, disapprove. (*My* stories don't have famous people in them.) I did the same thing with my father's drunken fiddler, Uncle Earl, once I learned he didn't exist. I used the story as a clue to help unravel the puzzle of my father's dreadful psychology, hoping no doubt to unravel the puzzle of my own.

One of the most difficult things to say to another person is I hope you will love me. Yet that is what we all want to say to one another— to our children, to our parents and mates, to our friends and even to strangers.

Perhaps especially to strangers. My friend in Boston, who joked with me about Sonny Tufts as an interlude in the story of her mother's awful dying, was showing me her hope that I would love her, even when the story itself was about her mother's lifelong refusal to love her and, with the woman's death, the absolute removal of any possibility of that love. I have, at least, my father's story of how I got my name, and though it's too late for me now to give him what, for a glimmering moment, he hoped and asked for, by remembering his story I have understood a little more usefully the telling of my own.

By remembering, as if writing my memoirs, what the stories of others have reminded me of, what they have literally brought to my mind, I have learned how my own stories function in the world, whether I tell them to my mother, to my wife, to my children, to my friends or, especially, to strangers. And to complete the circle, I have learned a little more usefully how to listen to the stories of others, whether they are true or not.

As I was leaving my mother that morning to drive back to Los Angeles and then fly home to New Hampshire, where my brother and sister and all my mother's grandchildren live and where all but the last few years of my mother's past was lived, she told me a new story. We stood in the shade of palm trees in the parking lot outside her glass-and-metal building for a few minutes, and she said to me in a concerned way, "You know that restaurant, the Pancake House, where you took me for breakfast this morning?"

I said yes and checked the time and flipped my suitcase into the back seat of the rented car.

"Well, I always have breakfast there on Wednesdays, it's on the way to where I baby-sit on Wednesdays, and this week something funny happened there. I sat alone way in the back, where they have that long, curving booth, and I didn't notice until I was halfway through my breakfast that at the far end of the booth a man was sitting there. He was maybe your age, a young man, but dirty and shabby. Especially dirty, and so I just looked away and went on eating my eggs and toast."

"But then I noticed he was looking at me, as if he knew me and didn't quite dare talk to me. I smiled, because maybe I did know him, I know just about everybody in the neighborhood now. But he was a stranger. And dirty. And I could see that he had been drinking for days."

"So I smiled and said to him, 'You want help, mister, don't you?'" He needed a shave, and his clothes were filthy and all ripped, and his hair was a mess. You know the type. But something pathetic about his eyes made me want to talk to him. But honestly, Earl, I couldn't. I just couldn't. He was so dirty and all."

"Anyhow, when I spoke to him, just that little bit, he sort of came out of his daze and sat up straight for a second, like he was afraid I was going to complain to the manager and have him thrown out of the restaurant. 'What did you say to me?' he asked. His voice was weak but he was trying to make it sound strong, so it came out kind of loud and broken. 'Nothing,' I said, and I turned away from him and quickly finished my breakfast and left."

"That afternoon, when I was walking back home from my baby-sitting job, I went into the restaurant to see if he was there, but he wasn't. And the next morning, Thursday, I walked all the way over there to check again, even though I never eat breakfast at the Pancake House on Thursdays, but he was gone then too. And then yesterday, Friday, I went back a third time. But he was gone." She lapsed into a thoughtful silence and looked at her hands.

40 "Was he there this morning?" I asked, thinking coincidence was 40 somehow the point of the story.

"No," she said. "But I didn't expect him to be there this morning. I'd stopped looking for him by yesterday."

"Well, why'd you tell me the story, then? What's it about?"

"About? Why, I don't know. Nothing, I guess. I just felt sorry for the man, and then because I was afraid, I shut up and left him alone." She was still studying her tiny hands.

"That's natural," I said. "You shouldn't feel guilty for that," I said, and I put my arms around her.

45 She turned her face into my shoulder. "I know, I know. But 45 still . . ." Her blue eyes filled, her son was leaving again, gone for another six months or a year, and who would she tell her stories to while he was gone? Who would listen?

The Fish

Elizabeth Bishop

Elizabeth Bishop was born in Worcester, Massachusetts, in 1911 and died in 1979. Her father died when she was eight months old, and her mother was confined to a mental institution when she was four years old. After a childhood further complicated by chronic asthma, she was graduated from Vassar in 1934 with a B.A., served as the Consultant in Poetry to the Library of Congress and beginning in 1951, she lived in Brazil for more than twenty years. In 1956, her book of poems North & South—A Cold Spring *won the Pulitzer prize. She also won the National Book Award and the National Book Critics Circle Award. In this poem, from her collection entitled simply* North and South *(1946) she addresses the subject of the eternal conflict between humans and nature.*

1   I caught a tremendous fish   1
and held him beside the boat
half out of water, with my hook
fast in a corner of his mouth.
5   He didn't fight.   5
He hadn't fought at all.
He hung a grunting weight,
battered and venerable
and homely. Here and there
10   his brown skin hung in strips   10
like ancient wallpaper,
and its pattern of darker brown
was like wallpaper:
shapes like full-blown roses

15   stained and lost through age.
He was speckled with barnacles,
fine rosettes of lime,
and infested
with tiny white sea-lice,
20   and underneath two or three
rags of green weed hung down.
While his gills were breathing in
the terrible oxygen
—the frightening gills,
25   fresh and crisp with blood,
that can cut so badly—
I thought of the coarse white flesh
packed in like feathers,
the big bones and the little bones
30   the dramatic reds and blacks
of his shiny entrails,
and the pink swim-bladder
like a big peony.
I looked into his eyes
35   which were far larger than mine
but shallower, and yellowed,
the irises backed and packed
with tarnished tinfoil
seen through the lenses
40   of old scratched isinglass.
They shifted a little, but not
to return my stare.
—It was more like the tipping
of an object toward the light.
45   I admired his sullen face,
the mechanism of his jaw,
and then I saw
that from his lower lip
—if you could call it a lip—
50   grim, wet, and weaponlike,
hung five old pieces of fish-line,
or four and a wire leader
with the swivel still attached,

with all their five big hooks
55 grown firmly in his mouth.
A green line, frayed at the end
where he broke it, two heavier lines,
and a fine black thread
still crimped from the strain and snap
60 when it broke and he got away.
Like medals with their ribbons
frayed and wavering,
a five-haired beard of wisdom
trailing from his aching jaw.
65 I stared and stared
and victory filled up
the little rented boat,
from the pool of bilge
where oil had spread a rainbow
70 around the rusted engine
to the bailer rusted orange,
the sun-cracked thwarts,
the oarlocks on their strings,
the gunnels—until everything
75 was, rainbow, rainbow, rainbow!
And I let the fish go.

Sign for My Father, Who Stressed the Bunt

David Bottoms

Poet David Bottoms was born in Canton, Georgia, in 1949. He lives in Atlanta and teaches at Georgia State University. In addition to publishing individual poems in magazines such as the Atlantic Monthly, Harper's, *the* Kenyon Review, *the* New Yorker, *the* Paris Review, *and the* Southern Review, *he has published several volumes of poetry. His first,* Shooting Rats at the Bibb County Dump, *won the Walt Whitman Award for a first book of poetry in 1980. His other collections include* In a U-Haul North of Damascus *(1983),* Under the Vulture-Tree *(1987),* Armored Hearts: Selected and New Poems *(1995), and* Vagrant Grace: Poems *(1999). He has also published two novels,* Easter Weekend *(1990) and* Any Cold Jordan *(1988). Among the many awards he has received are the Levinson Prize, the Ingram-Merril Award, and a National Endowment for the Arts Fellowship. In this poem, originally published in his second collection, Bottoms uses a baseball metaphor to comment on life lessons passed on from father to son.*

1   On the rough diamond,
     the hand-cut field below the dog lot and barn,
     we rehearsed the strict technique
     of bunting. I watched from the infield,
5   the mound, the backstop

as your left hand climbed the bat, your legs
and shoulders squared toward the pitcher.
You could drop it like a seed
down either base line. I admired your style,
10 but not enough to take my eyes off the bank
that served as our center-field fence.

Years passed, three leagues of organized ball,
no few lives. I could homer
into the garden beyond the bank,
15 into the left-field lot of Carmichael Motors,
and still you stressed the same technique,
the crouch and spring, the lead arm absorbing
just enough impact. That whole tiresome pitch
about basics never changing,
20 and I never learned what you were laying down.
Like a hand brushed across the bill of a cap,
let this be the sign
I'm getting a grip on the sacrifice.

There Will Come Soft Rains

Ray Bradbury

Ray Douglas Bradbury (1920–) was born in Waukegan, Illinois. A storywriter and novelist, a playwright, a screenwriter, and a poet, Bradbury is one of the most distinguished and beloved science fiction writers. In 1934, Bradbury moved to Los Angeles, California where he met such famous people as the great comedian, George Burns, who paid Bradbury for his very first work—a joke for Burns's comedy show. In 1947 Bradbury published his first collection of short stories, Dark Carnival. The Martian Chronicles *(1950), in which he imagined humans colonizing Mars, made him famous. In 1953* Fahrenheit 451 *struck a darker note as it imagined a world where books were burned and ideas suppressed. Bradbury has won the O. Henry Memorial Award; the Benjamin Franklin Award (1954); the Aviation-Space Writer's Association Award for Best Space Article in an American Magazine (1967); and the World Fantasy Award for Lifetime Achievement. His work was included in the* Best American Short Stories *collections for 1946, 1948, and 1952. Bradbury's most unusual honor came when an Apollo astronaut named Dandelion Crater on the moon after Bradbury's novel,* Dandelion Wine.*

"There Will Come Soft Rains" was first published in* Colliers *magazine on May 6, 1950. The story revolves around a house that was built to withstand nuclear blasts and to run itself for human convenience. In the story the* *house stands, but the family is burned into the outer wall by a blast. The tale ends with the house reading Sara Teasedale's poem about the world without humans.*

1 In the living room the voice-clock sang, *Tick-tock, seven o'clock, time to get up, time to get up, seven o'clock!* as if it were afraid that nobody would. The morning house lay empty. The clock ticked on, repeating and repeating its sounds into the emptiness. *Seven-nine, breakfast time, seven-nine!*

In the kitchen the breakfast stove gave a hissing sigh and ejected from its warm interior eight pieces of perfectly browned toast, eight eggs sunnyside up, sixteen slices of bacon, two coffees, and two cool glasses of milk.

"Today is August 4, 2026," said a second voice from the kitchen ceiling, "in the city of Allendale, California." It repeated the date three times for memory's sake. "Today is Mr. Featherstone's birthday. Today is the anniversary of Tilita's marriage. Insurance is payable, as are the water, gas, and light bills."

Somewhere in the walls, relays clicked, memory tapes glided under electric eyes.

5 *Eight-one, tick-tock, eight-one o'clock, off to school, off to work, run, run, eight-one!* But no doors slammed, no carpets took the soft tread of rubber heels. It was raining outside. The weather box on the front door sang quietly: "Rain, rain, go away; rubbers, raincoats for today . . ." And the rain tapped on the empty house, echoing.

Outside, the garage chimed and lifted its door to reveal the waiting car. After a long wait the door swung down again.

At eight-thirty the eggs were shriveled and the toast was like stone. An aluminum wedge scraped them into the sink, where hot water whirled them down a metal throat which digested and flushed them away to the distant sea. The dirty dishes were dropped into a hot washer and emerged twinkling dry.

Nine-fifteen, sang the clock, *time to clean.*

Out of warrens in the wall, tiny robot mice darted. The rooms were acrawl with the small cleaning animals, all rubber and metal. They thudded against chairs, whirling their mustached runners, kneading the rug nap, sucking gently at hidden dust. Then, like mysterious invaders, they popped into their burrows. Their pink electric eyes faded. The house was clean.

Ten o'clock. The sun came out from behind the rain. The house stood alone in a city of rubble and ashes. This was the one house left standing. At night the ruined city gave off a radioactive glow which could be seen for miles.

Ten-fifteen. The garden sprinklers whirled up in golden founts, filling the soft morning air with scatterings of brightness. The water pelted windowpanes, running down the charred west side where the house had been burned evenly free of its white paint. The entire west face of the house was black, save for five places. Here the silhouette in paint of a man mowing a lawn. Here, as in a photograph, a woman bent to pick flowers. Still farther over, their images burned on wood in one titanic instant, a small boy, hands flung into the air; higher up, the image of a thrown ball, and opposite him a girl, hands raised to catch a ball which never came down.

The five spots of paint—the man, the woman, the children, the ball—remained. The rest was a thin charcoaled layer.

The gentle sprinkler rain filled the garden with falling light.

Until this day, how well the house had kept its peace. How carefully it had inquired, "Who goes there? What's the password?" and, getting no answer from lonely foxes and whining cats, it had shut up its windows and drawn shades in an old- maidenly preoccupation with self-protection which bordered on a mechanical paranoia.

It quivered at each sound, the house did. If a sparrow brushed a window, the shade shapped up. The bird, startled, flew off! No, not even a bird must touch the house!

The house was an altar with ten thousand attendants, big, small, servicing, attending, in choirs. But the gods had gone away, and the ritual of the religion continued senselessly, uselessly.

Twelve noon.

A dog whined, shivering, on the front porch.

The front door recognized the dog voice and opened. The dog, once huge and fleshy, but now gone to bone and covered with sores, moved in and through the house, tracking mud. Behind it whirred angry mice, angry at having to pick up mud, angry at inconvenience.

For not a leaf fragment blew under the door but what the wall panels flipped open and the copper scrap rats flashed swiftly out. The offending dust, hair, or paper, seized in miniature steel jaws, was raced back to the burrows. There, down tubes which fed into the cellar, it was dropped into the sighing vent of an incinerator which sat like evil Baal in a dark corner.

The dog ran upstairs, hysterically yelping to each door, at last realizing, as the house realized, that only silence was here.

It sniffed the air and scratched the kitchen door. Behind the door, the stove was making pancakes which filled the house with a rich baked odor and the scent of maple syrup.

The dog frothed at the mouth, lying at the door, sniffing, its eyes turned to fire. It ran wildly in circles, biting at its tail, spun in a frenzy, and died. It lay in the parlor for an hour.

Two o'clock, sang a voice.

25 Delicately sensing decay at last, the regiments of mice hummed out as softly as blown gray leaves in an electrical wind. 25

Two-fifteen.

The dog was gone.

In the cellar, the incinerator glowed suddenly and a whirl of sparks leaped up the chimney.

Two thirty-five.

30 Bridge tables sprouted from patio walls. Playing cards fluttered onto pads in a shower of pips. Martinis manifested on an oaken bench with egg-salad sandwiches. Music played. 30

But the tables were silent and the cards untouched.

At four o'clock the tables folded like great butterflies back through the paneled walls.

Four-thirty.

The nursery walls glowed.

35 Animals took shape: yellow giraffes, blue lions, pink antelopes, lilac panthers cavorting in crystal substance. The walls were glass. They looked out upon color and fantasy. Hidden films clocked through well-oiled sprockets, and the walls lived. The nursery floor was woven to resemble a crisp, cereal meadow. Over this ran aluminum roaches and iron crickets, and in the hot still air butterflies of delicate red tissue wavered among the sharp aroma of animal spoors! There was the sound like a great matted yellow hive of bees within a dark bellows, the lazy bumble of a purring lion. And there was the patter of okapi feet and the murmur of a fresh jungle rain, like other 35

hoofs, falling upon the summer-starched grass. Now the walls dissolved into distances of parched weed, mile on mile, and warm endless sky. The animals drew away into thorn brakes and water holes.

It was the children's hour.

Five o'clock. The bath filled with clear hot water.

Six, seven, eight o'clock. The dinner dishes manipulated like magic tricks, and in the study a *click.* In the metal stand opposite the hearth where a fire now blazed up warmly, a cigar popped out, half an inch of soft gray ash on it, smoking, waiting.

Nine o'clock. The beds warmed their hidden circuits, for nights were cool here.

Nine-five. A voice spoke from the study ceiling:

"Mrs. McClellan, which poem would you like this evening?"

The house was silent.

The voice said at last, "Since you express no preference, I shall select a poem at random." Quiet music rose to back the voice. "Sara Teasdale. As I recall, your favorite. . . .

"There will come soft rains and the smell of the ground,
And swallows circling with their shimmering sound;

And frogs in the pools singing at night,
And wild plum trees in tremulous white;

Robins will wear their feathery fire,
Whistling their whims on a low fence-wire;

And not one will know of the war, not one
Will care at last when it is done.

Not one would mind, neither bird nor tree,
If mankind perished utterly;

And Spring herself, when she woke at dawn
Would scarcely know that we were gone."

The fire burned on the stone hearth and the cigar fell away into a mound of quiet ash on its tray. The empty chairs faced each other between the silent walls, and the music played.

45   At ten o'clock the house began to die.

The wind blew. A falling tree bough crashed through the kitchen window. Cleaning solvent, bottled, shattered over the stove. The room was ablaze in an instant!

"Fire!" screamed a voice. The house lights flashed, water pumps shot water from the ceilings. But the solvent spread on the linoleum, licking, eating, under the kitchen door, while the voices took it up in chorus: "Fire, fire, fire!"

The house tried to save itself. Doors sprang tightly shut, but the windows were broken by the heat and the wind blew and sucked upon the fire.

The house gave ground as the fire in ten billion angry sparks moved with flaming ease from room to room and then up the stairs. While scurrying water rats squeaked from the walls, pistoled their water, and ran for more. And the wall sprays let down showers of mechanical rain.

50   But too late. Somewhere, sighing, a pump shrugged to a stop. The quenching rain ceased. The reserve water supply which had filled baths and washed dishes for many quiet days was gone.

The fire crackled up the stairs. It fed upon Picassos and Matisses in the upper halls, like delicacies, baking off the oily flesh, tenderly crisping the canvases into black shavings.

Now the fire lay in beds, stood in windows, changed the colors of drapes!

And then, reinforcements.

From attic trapdoors, blind robot faces peered down with faucet mouths gushing green chemical.

55   The fire backed off, as even an elephant must at the sight of a dead snake. Now there were twenty snakes whipping over the floor, killing the fire with a clear cold venom of green froth.

But the fire was clever. It had sent flames outside the house, up through the attic to the pumps there. An explosion! The attic brain which directed the pumps was shattered into bronze shrapnel on the beams.

The fire rushed back into every closet and felt of the clothes hung there.

The house shuddered, oak bone on bone, its bared skeleton cringing from the heat, its wire, its nerves revealed as if a surgeon had torn the skin off to let the red veins and capillaries quiver in the scalded air. Help, help! Fire! Run, run! Heat snapped mirrors like the brittle winter ice. And the voices wailed Fire, fire, run, run, like a tragic nursery rhyme, a dozen voices, high, low, like children dying in a forest, alone, alone. And the voices fading as the wires popped their sheathings like hot chestnuts. One, two, three, four, five voices died.

In the nursery the jungle burned. Blue lions roared, purple giraffes bounded off. The panthers ran in circles, changing color, and ten million animals, running before the fire, vanished off toward a distant steaming river. . . .

60 Ten more voices died. In the last instant under the fire avalanche, 60 other choruses, oblivious, could be heard announcing the time, playing music, cutting the lawn by remote-control mower, or setting an umbrella frantically out and in the slamming and opening front door, a thousand things happening, like a clock shop when each clock strikes the hour insanely before or after the other, a scene of maniac confusion, yet unity; singing, screaming, a few last cleaning mice darting bravely out to carry the horrid ashes away! And one voice, with sublime disregard for the situation, read poetry aloud in the fiery study, until all the film spools burned, until all the wires withered and the circuits cracked.

The fire burst the house and let it slam flat down, puffing out skirts of spark and smoke.

In the kitchen, an instant before the rain of fire and timber, the stove could be seen making breakfasts at a psychopathic rate, ten dozen eggs, six loaves of toast, twenty dozen bacon strips, which, eaten by fire, started the stove working again, hysterically hissing!

The crash. The attic smashing into kitchen and parlor. The parlor into cellar, cellar into sub-cellar. Deep freeze, armchair, film tapes, circuits, beds, and all like skeletons thrown in a cluttered mound deep under.

Smoke and silence. A great quantity of smoke.

65 Dawn showed faintly in the east. Among the ruins, one wall 65 stood alone. Within the wall, a last voice said, over and over again and again, even as the sun rose to shine upon the heaped rubble and steam:

"Today is August 5, 2026, today is August 5, 2026, today is . . ."

We Real Cool

Gwendolyn Brooks

Gwendolyn Brooks (1917-) was born in Topeka, Kansas, but has lived her life in Chicago and has become one of the most beloved of Illinois poets. She attended Wilson Junior College in Chicago and was graduated in 1938. Her first poem, "Eventide," appeared in the magazine American Childhood *when she was yet in her early teens. She published many poems in the* Chicago Defender, *a local paper. Her first book of poems,* A Street in Bronzeville *was published in 1945.* Annie Allen *(1949) won Brooks a Pulitzer Prize. Other collections of her poetry include* Bronzeville Boy and Girls *(1956),* The Bean Eaters *(1960),* Selected Poems *(1963),* In the Mecca *(1968),* Riot *(1969),* Blacks *(1987), and* Children Coming Home *(1991). She also has written an autobiographical novel,* Maud Martha *(1953) and a book of memoirs,* Report from Part One *(1972). "We Real Cool" expresses the quality of life in the city for young African-American men in the early 1960s.*

The Pool Players.
Seven at the Golden Shovel.

1   We real cool. We
     Left school. We

     Lurk late. We
     Strike straight. We

     Sing sin. We
     Thin gin. We

     Jazz June. We
     Die soon.

The Myth of Sisyphus

Albert Camus

Albert Camus (1913–1960) was born in Mondovi, Algeria (at that time a colony of France). Camus attended the University of Algeria, where he majored in philosophy. He wrote for the Alger-Republicain, *a socialist paper, between 1937 and 1939, and edited* Soir-Republicain, *another socialist paper, from 1939–1940. He moved to France during World War II, joined the Resistance, and wrote for and edited the underground publication* Combat. *A leading proponent of existentialism, Camus is perhaps best remembered for* The Rebel: An Essay on Man in Revolt *(1954), for which he received the Nobel Prize for Literature (1957). Other books by Camus include* The Myth of Sisyphus *(1942), his first collection of philosophical essays, and the novels* The Stranger *(1942),* The Plague *(1947),* The Fall *(1956), and* Exile and the Kingdom *(1957). In this story, Camus analyzes the meaning and impact of the fate of Sisyphus—a symbol of the human condition.*

1   The gods had condemned Sisyphus to ceaselessly rolling a rock to the top of a mountain, whence the stone would fall back of its own weight. They had thought with some reason that there is no more dreadful punishment than futile and hopeless labor.

If one believes Homer, Sisyphus was the wisest and most prudent of mortals. According to another tradition, however, he was disposed to practice the profession of highwayman. I see no contradiction in this. Opinions differ as to the reasons why he became the futile laborer of the underworld. To begin with, he is accused of a certain levity in regard to the gods. He stole their secrets. Aegina, the daughter of

Aesopus, was carried off by Jupiter. The father was shocked by that disappearance and complained to Sisyphus. He, who knew of the abduction, offered to tell about it on condition that Aesopus would give water to the citadel of Corinth. To the celestial thunderbolts he preferred the benediction of water. He was punished for this in the underworld. Homer tells us also that Sisyphus had put Death in chains. Pluto could not endure the sight of his deserted, silent empire. He dispatched the god of war, who liberated Death from the hands of her conqueror.

It is said also that Sisyphus, being near to death, rashly wanted to test his wife's love. He ordered her to cast his unburied body into the middle of the public square. Sisyphus woke up in the underworld. And there, annoyed by an obedience so contrary to human love, he obtained from Pluto permission to return to earth in order to chastise his wife. But when he had seen again the face of this world, enjoyed water and sun, warm stones and the sea, he no longer wanted to go back to the infernal darkness. Recalls, signs of anger, warnings were of no avail. Many years more he lived facing the curve of the gulf, the sparkling sea, and the smiles of earth. A decree of the gods was necessary. Mercury came and seized the impudent man by the collar and, snatching him from his joys, led him forcibly back to the underworld, where his rock was ready for him.

You have already grasped that Sisyphus is the absurd hero. He *is,* as much through his passions as through his torture. His scorn of the gods, his hatred of death, and his passion for life won him that unspeakable penalty in which the whole being is exerted toward accomplishing nothing. This is the price that must be paid for the passions of this earth. Nothing is told us about Sisyphus in the underworld. Myths are made for the imagination to breathe life into them. As for this myth, one sees merely the whole effort of a body straining to raise the huge stone, to roll it and push it up a slope a hundred times over; one sees the face screwed up, the cheek tight against the stone, the shoulder bracing the clay-covered mass, the foot wedging it, the fresh start with arms outstretched, the wholly human security of two earth-clotted hands. At the very end of his long effort measured by skyless space and time without depth, the purpose is achieved. Then Sisyphus watches the stone rush down in a few moments toward that lower world whence he will have to push it up again toward the summit. He goes back down to the plain.

It is during that return, that pause, that Sisyphus interests me. A face that toils so close to stones is already stone itself! I see that man going back down with a heavy yet measured step toward the torment of which he will never know the end. That hour like a breathing-space which returns as surely as his suffering, that is the hour of consciousness. At each of those moments when he leaves the heights and gradually sinks toward the lairs of the gods, he is superior to his fate. He is stronger than his rock.

If this myth is tragic, that is because its hero is conscious. Where would his torture be, indeed, if at every step the hope of succeeding upheld him? The workman of today works every day in his life at the same tasks, and his fate is no less absurd. But it is tragic only at the rare moments when it becomes conscious. Sisyphus, proletarian of the gods, powerless and rebellious, knows the whole extent of his wretched condition: it is what he thinks of during his descent. The lucidity that was to constitute his torture at the same time crowns his victory. There is no fate that cannot be surmounted by scorn.

If the descent is thus sometimes performed in sorrow, it can also take place in joy. This word is not too much. Again I fancy Sisyphus returning toward his rock, and the sorrow was in the beginning. When the images of earth cling too tightly to memory, when the call of happiness becomes too insistent, it happens that melancholy rises in man's heart: this is the rock's victory, this is the rock itself. The boundless grief is too heavy to bear. These are our nights of Gethsemane. But crushing truths perish from being acknowledged. Thus, Oedipus at the outset obeys fate without knowing it. But from the moment he knows, his tragedy begins. Yet at the same moment, blind and desperate, he realizes that the only bond linking him to the world is the cool hand of a girl. Then a tremendous remark rings out: "Despite so many ordeals, my advanced age and the nobility of my soul make me conclude that all is well." Sophocles' Oedipus, like Dostoevsky's Kirilov, thus gives the recipe for the absurd victory. Ancient wisdom confirms modern heroism.

One does not discover the absurd without being tempted to write a manual of happiness. "What! by such narrow ways—?" There is but one world, however. Happiness and the absurd are two sons of the same earth. They are inseparable. It would be a mistake to say that happiness necessarily springs from the absurd discovery. It happens as well that the feeling of the absurd springs from happiness. "I conclude that all is well," says Oedipus, and that remark is sacred. It echoes in the wild and limited universe of man. It teaches that all is not, has not been, exhausted. It drives out of this world a god who had come into it with dissatisfaction and a preference for futile sufferings. It makes of fate a human matter, which must be settled among men.

All Sisyphus' silent joy is contained therein. His fate belongs to him. His rock is his thing. Likewise, the absurd man, when he contemplates his torment, silences all the idols. In the universe suddenly restored to its silence, the myriad wondering little voices of the earth rise up. Unconscious, secret calls, invitations from all the faces, they are the necessary reverse and price of victory. There is no sun without shadow, and it is essential to know the night. The absurd man says yes and his effort will henceforth be unceasing. If there is a personal fate, there is no higher destiny, or at least there is but one which he concludes is inevitable and despicable. For the rest, he knows himself to be the master of his days. At that subtle moment when man glances backward over his life, Sisyphus returning toward his rock, in that slight pivoting he contemplates that series of unrelated actions which becomes his fate, created by him, combined under his memory's eye and soon sealed by his death. Thus, convinced of the wholly human origin of all that is human, a blind man eager to see who knows that the night has no end, he is still on the go. The rock is still rolling.

10 I leave Sisyphus at the foot of the mountain! One always finds 10 one's burden again. But Sisyphus teaches the higher fidelity that negates the gods and raises rocks. He too concludes that all is well. This universe henceforth without a master seems to him neither sterile nor futile. Each atom of that stone, each mineral flake of that night-filled mountain, in itself forms a world. The struggle itself toward the heights is enough to fill a man's heart. One must imagine Sisyphus happy.

The Storm

Kate Chopin

Kate Chopin (b. Katherine O'Flaherty, 1851–1904) began her life in St. Louis, Missouri. Her father died when she was four years old, so she was reared by three widows: her mother, her grandmother, and her great-grandmother. She graduated from Sacred Heart convent in 1870 and then married Oscar Chopin, following him to New Orleans and later to his plantation in northern Louisiana. The mother of six children, she was widowed in 1882 and moved back to St. Louis where she began to write stories and publish in stylish literary magazines. Her novels, At Fault *(1890) and* The Awakening *(1899), shocked conservative Victorian society but are praised by modern critics. Her collections of short stories,* Bayou Folk *(1894) and* A Night in Acadie *(1897), draw on her years of experience on a Louisiana plantation among Creole people. She died of a brain hemmorage at only fifty-three. In "The Storm" Chopin exlpores the unpredictable results of an adulterous encounter between two former sweethearts during a sudden, violent storm.*

I

1   The leaves were so still that even Bibi thought it was going to rain. Bobinôt, who was accustomed to converse on terms of perfect equality with his little son, called the child's attention to certain somber clouds that were rolling with sinister intention from the west, accompanied by a sullen, threatening roar. They were at

---

The Storm (1898)

Friedheimer's store and decided to remain there till the storm had passed. They sat within the door on two empty kegs. Bibi was four years old and looked very wise.

"Mama'll be 'fraid, yes," he suggested with blinking eyes.

"She'll shut the house. Maybe she got Sylvie helpin' her this evenin'," Bobinôt responded reassuringly.

"No; she ent got Sylvie. Sylvie was helpin' her yistiday," piped Bibi.

5   Bobinôt arose and going across to the counter purchased a can of shrimps, of which Calixta was very fond. Then he returned to his perch on the keg and sat stolidly holding the can of shrimps while the storm burst. It shook the wooden store and seemed to be ripping great furrows in the distant field. Bibi laid his little hand on his father's knee and was not afraid.

II

Calixta, at home, felt no uneasiness for their safety. She sat at a side window sewing furiously on a sewing machine. She was greatly occupied and did not notice the approaching storm. But she felt very warm and often stopped to mop her face on which the perspiration gathered in beads. She unfastened her white sacque at the throat. It began to grow dark, and suddenly realizing the situation she got up hurriedly and went about closing windows and doors.

Out on the small front gallery she had hung Bobinôt's Sunday clothes to air and she hastened out to gather them before the rain fell. As she stepped outside, Alcée Laballière rode in at the gate. She had not seen him very often since her marriage, and never alone. She stood there with Bobinôt's coat in her hands, and the big rain drops began to fall. Alcée rode his horse under the shelter of a side projection where the chickens had huddled and there were plows and a harrow piled up in the corner.

"May I come and wait on your gallery till the storm is over, Calixta?" he asked.

"Come 'long in, M'sieur Alcée."

10   His voice and her own startled her as if from a trance, and she seized Bobinôt's vest. Alcée, mounting to the porch, grabbed the trousers and snatched Bibi's braided jacket that was about to be carried away by a sudden gust of wind. He expressed an intention to re-

main outside, but it was soon apparent that he might as well have been out in the open: the water beat in upon the boards in driving sheets, and he went inside, closing the door after him. It was even necessary to put something beneath the door to keep the water out.

"My! what a rain! It's good two years since it rain' like that," exclaimed Calixta as she rolled up a piece of bagging and Alcée helped her to thrust it beneath the crack.

She was a little fuller of figure than five years before when she married; but she had lost nothing of her vivacity. Her blue eyes still retained their melting quality; and her yellow hair, dishevelled by the wind and rain, kinked more stubbornly than ever about her ears and temples.

The rain beat upon the low, shingled roof with a force and clatter that threatened to break an entrance and deluge them there. They were in the dining room—the sitting room—the general utility room. Adjoining was her bed room, with Bibi's couch along side her own. The door stood open, and the room with its white, monumental bed, its closed shutters, looked dim and mysterious.

Alcée flung himself into a rocker and Calixta nervously began to gather up from the floor the lengths of a cotton sheet which she had been sewing.

15   "If this keeps up, *Dieu sait* if the levees goin' to stan' it!" she exclaimed.   15

"What have you got to do with the levees?"

"I got enough to do! An' there's Bobinôt with Bibi out in that storm—if he only didn' left Friedheimer's!"

"Let us hope, Calixta, that Bobinôt's got sense enough to come in out of a cyclone."

She went and stood at the window with a greatly disturbed look on her face. She wiped the frame that was clouded with moisture. It was stiflingly hot. Alcée got up and joined her at the window, looking over her shoulder. The rain was coming down in sheets obscuring the view of far-off cabins and enveloping the distant wood in a gray mist. The playing of the lightning was incessant. A bolt struck a tall chinaberry tree at the edge of the field. It filled all visible space with a blinding glare and the crash seemed to invade the very boards they stood upon.

20   Calixta put her hands to her eyes, and with a cry, staggered backward. Alcée's arm encircled her, and for an instant he drew her close and spasmodically to him.   20

"Bonté!" she cried, releasing herself from his encircling arm and retreating from the window, "the house'll go next! If I only knew w'ere Bibi was!" She would not compose herself; she would not be seated. Alcée clasped her shoulders and looked into her face. The contact of her warm, palpitating body when he had unthinkingly drawn her into his arms, had aroused all the old-time infatuation and desire for her flesh.

"Calixta," he said, "don't be frightened. Nothing can happen. The house is too low to be struck, with so many tall trees standing about. There! aren't you going to be quiet? say, aren't you?" He pushed her hair back from her face that was warm and steaming. Her lips were as red and moist as pomegranate seed. Her white neck and a glimpse of her full, firm bosom disturbed him powerfully. As she glanced up at him the fear in her liquid blue eyes had given place to a drowsy gleam that unconsciously betrayed a sensuous desire. He looked down into her eyes and there was nothing for him to do but to gather her lips in a kiss. It reminded him of Assumption.

"Do you remember—in Assumption, Calixta?" he asked in a low voice broken by passion. Oh! she remembered; for in Assumption he had kissed her and kissed and kissed her; until his senses would well nigh fail, and to save her he would resort to a desperate flight. If she was not an immaculate dove in those days, she was still inviolate; a passionate creature whose very defenselessness had made her defense, against which his honor forbade him to prevail. Now—well, now— her lips seemed in a manner free to be tasted, as well as her round, white throat and her whiter breasts.

They did not heed the crashing torrents, and the roar of the elements made her laugh as she lay in his arms. She was a revelation in that dim, mysterious chamber; as white as the couch she lay upon. Her firm, elastic flesh that was knowing for the first time its birthright, was like a creamy lily that the sun invites to contribute its breath and perfume to the undying life of the world.

25   The generous abundance of her passion, without guile or trickery,   25
was like a white flame which penetrated and found response in depths of his own sensuous nature that had never yet been reached.

When he touched her breasts they gave themselves up in quivering ecstasy, inviting his lips. Her mouth was a fountain of delight. And when he possessed her, they seemed to swoon together at the very borderland of life's mystery.

He stayed cushioned upon her, breathless, dazed, enervated, with his heart beating like a hammer upon her. With one hand she clasped his head, her lips lightly touching his forehead. The other hand stroked with a soothing rhythm his muscular shoulders.

The growl of the thunder was distant and passing away. The rain beat softly upon the shingles, inviting them to drowsiness and sleep. But they dared not yield.

The rain was over; and the sun was turning the glistening green world into a palace of gems. Calixta, on the gallery, watched Alcée ride away. He turned and smiled at her with a beaming face; and she lifted her pretty chin in the air and laughed aloud.

III

30 Bobinôt and Bibi, trudging home, stopped without at the cistern to 30 make themselves presentable.

"My! Bibi, w'at will yo' mama say! You ought to be ashame'. You oughtn' put on those good pants. Look at 'em! An' that mud on yo' collar! How you got that mud on yo' collar, Bibi? I never saw such a boy!" Bibi was the picture of pathetic resignation. Bobinôt was the embodiment of serious solicitude as he strove to remove from his own person and his son's the signs of their tramp over heavy roads and through wet fields. He scraped the mud off Bibi's bare legs and feet with a stick and carefully removed all traces from his heavy brogans. Then, prepared for the worst—the meeting with an over-scrupulous housewife, they entered cautiously at the back door.

Calixta was preparing supper. She had set the table and was dripping coffee at the hearth. She sprang up as they came in.

"Oh, Bobinôt! You back! My! but I was uneasy. W'ere you been during the rain? An' Bibi? he ain't wet? he ain't hurt?" She had clasped Bibi and was kissing him effusively. Bobinôt's explanations and apologies which he had been composing all along the way, died on his lips as Calixta felt him to see if he were dry, and seemed to express nothing but satisfaction at their safe return.

"I brought you some shrimps, Calixta," offered Bobinôt, hauling the can from his ample side pocket and laying it on the table.

35 "Shrimps! Oh, Bobinôt! you too good fo' anything!" and she gave 35 him a smacking kiss on the cheek that resounded. *"J'vous reponds,'* we'll have a feas' to-night! umph-umph!"

Bobinôt and Bibi began to relax and enjoy themselves, and when the three seated themselves at table they laughed much and so loud that anyone might have heard them as far away as Laballière's.

IV

Alcée Laballière wrote to his wife, Clarisse, that night. It was a loving letter, full of tender solictude. He told her not to hurry back, but if she and the babies liked it at Biloxi, to stay a month longer. He was getting on nicely; and though he missed them, he was willing to bear the separation a while longer—realizing that their health and pleasure were the first things to be considered.

V

As for Clarisse, she was charmed upon receiving her husband's letter. She and the babies were doing well. The society was agreeable; many of her old friends and acquaintances were at the bay. And the first free breath since her marriage seemed to restore the pleasant liberty of her maiden days. Devoted as she was to her husband, their intimate conjugal life was something which she was more than willing to forego for a while.

So the storm passed and everyone was happy.

The Story of an Hour

Kate Chopin

Kate Chopin (b. Katherine O'Flaherty, 1851–1904) began her life in St. Louis, Missouri. Her father died when she was four years old, so she was reared by three widows: her mother, her grandmother, and her great-grandmother. She was graduated from Sacred Heart convent in 1870 and then married Oscar Chopin, following him to New Orleans and later to his plantation in northern Louisiana. The mother of six children, she was widowed in 1882 and moved back to St. Louis where she began to write stories and publish in stylish literary magazines. Her novels, At Fault (1890) and The Awakening (1899), shocked conservative Victorian society but are praised by modern critics. Her collections of short stories, Bayou Folk (1894) and A Night in Acadie (1897) draw on her years of experience on a Louisiana plantation among Creole people. She died of a brain hemorrhage at only fifty-three. "The Story of an Hour" caused Chopin to be shunned by both her literary club and magazine publishers at the close of the nineteenth century, but it has persevered to become especially appealing to women in the late twentieth century.

1   Knowing that Mrs. Mallard was afflicted with a heart trouble, great care was taken to break to her as gently as possible the news of her husband's death.

It was her sister Josephine who told her, in broken sentences, veiled hints that revealed in half concealing. Her husband's friend Richards was there, too, near her. It was he who had been in the newspaper office when intelligence of the railroad disaster was received, with Brently Mallard's name leading the list of "killed." He had only taken the time to assure himself of its truth by a second telegram, and had hastened to forestall any less careful, less tender friend in bearing the sad message.

The Story of an Hour (1894)

She did not hear the story as many women have heard the same, with a paralyzed inability to accept its significance. She wept at once, with sudden, wild abandonment, in her sister's arms. When the storm of grief had spent itself she went away to her room alone. She would have no one follow her.

There stood, facing the open window, a comfortable, roomy arm-chair. Into this she sank, pressed down by a physical exhaustion that haunted her body and seemed to reach into her soul.

5   She could see in the open square before her house the tops of trees   5 that were all aquiver with the new spring life. The delicious breath of rain was in the air. In the street below a peddler was crying his wares. The notes of a distant song which someone was singing reached her faintly, and countless sparrows were twittering in the eaves.

There were patches of blue sky showing here and there through the clouds that had met and piled above the other in the west facing her window.

She sat with her head thrown back upon the cushion of the chair, quite motionless, except when a sob came up into her throat and shook her, as a child who has cried itself to sleep continues to sob in its dreams.

She was young, with a fair, calm face, whose lines bespoke re-pression and even a certain strength. But now there was a dull stare in her eyes, whose gaze was fixed away off yonder on one of those patches of blue sky. It was not a glance of reflection, but rather indicated a sus-pension of intelligent thought.

There was something coming to her and she was waiting for it, fearfully. What was it? She did not know; it was too subtle and elusive to name. But she felt it, creeping out of the sky, reaching toward her through the sounds, the scents, the color that filled the air.

10   Now her bosom rose and fell tumultuously. She was beginning to   10 recognize this thing that was approaching to possess her, and she was striving to beat it back with her will—as powerless as her two white slender hands would have been.

When she abandoned herself a little whispered word escaped her slightly parted lips. She said it over and over under her breath: "Free, free, free!" The vacant stare and the look of terror that had followed it went from her eyes. They stayed keen and bright. Her pulses beat fast, and the coursing blood warmed and relaxed every inch of her body.

She did not stop to ask if it were or were not a monstrous joy that held her. A clear and exalted perception enabled her to dismiss the suggestion as trivial.

She knew that she would weep again when she saw the kind, tender hands folded in death; the face that had never looked save with love upon her, fixed and gray and dead. But she saw beyond that bitter moment a long procession of years to come that would belong to her absolutely. And she opened and spread her arms out to them in welcome.

There would be no one to live for her during those coming years; she would live for herself. There would be no powerful will bending her in that blind persistence with which men and women believe they have a right to impose a private will upon a fellow-creature. A kind intention or a cruel intention made the act seem no less a crime as she looked upon it in that brief moment of illumination.

15   And yet she had loved him—sometimes. Often she had not. What   15
did it matter! What could love, the unsolved mystery, count for in face of this possession of self-assertion which she suddenly recognized as the strongest impulse of her being!

"Free! Body and soul free!" she kept whispering.

Josephine was kneeling before the closed door with her lips to the keyhole, imploring for admission. "Louise, open the door! I beg; open the door—you will make yourself ill. What are you doing, Louise? For heaven's sake open the door."

"Go away. I am not making myself ill." No; she was drinking in a very elixir of life through that open window.

Her fancy was running riot along those days ahead of her. Spring days, and summer days, and all sorts of days that would be her own. She breathed a quick prayer that life might be long. It was only yesterday she had thought with a shudder that life might be long.

20   She arose at length and opened the door to her sister's importu-   20
nities. There was a feverish triumph in her eyes, and she carried herself unwittingly like a goddess of Victory. She clasped her sister's waist, and together they descended the stairs. Richards stood waiting for them at the bottom.

Someone was opening the front door with a latchkey. It was Brently Mallard who entered, a little travel-stained, composedly carrying his grip-sack and umbrella. He had been far from the scene of accident, and did not even know there had been one. He stood amazed at Josephine's piercing cry; at Richards' quick motion to screen him from the view of his wife.

But Richards was too late.

When the doctors came they said she had died of heart disease— of joy that kills.

The Star

Arthur C. Clarke

Arthur Charles Clarke (1917–2008) was born in Minehead, England; was graduated with honors from King's College, London, in 1948; then taught radar during W.W.II. He turned from science to science fiction in 1951 with his first book, Prelude to Space. *He became the grand master of science fiction writing, having won scores of awards for his work. In the 1950s he moved to Sri Lanka where he remained for the rest of his life and continued to write such famous works as* 2001: A Space Odyssey *(1968) and* 3001: The Final Odyssey *(1997). His* Rendezvous with Rama *(1973) and* The Garden of Rama *(1991) ask some of the same philosophical questions as the more popular* Space Odyssey *collection. "The Star" demonstrates the profound philosophical complexities of Clarke's thinking.*

1   It is three thousand light-years to the Vatican. Once I believed that space could have no power over Faith. Just as I believed that the heavens declared the glory of God's handiwork. Now I have seen that handiwork, and my faith is sorely troubled.

I stare at the crucifix that hangs on the cabin wall above the Mark VI computer, and for the first time in my life I wonder if it is no more than an empty symbol.

I have told no one yet, but the truth cannot be concealed. The data are there for anyone to read, recorded on the countless miles of magnetic tape and the thousands of photographs we are carrying back to Earth. Other scientists can interpret them as easily as I can—more easily, in all probability. I am not one who would condone that

"The Star" by Arthur C. Clarke from *The Hugo Winners*, edited by Isaac Asimov and published by Doubleday, 1955. Reprinted with permission by the Scovil, Chicak & Galen Agency.

tampering with the Truth which often gave my Order a bad name in the olden days.

The crew is already sufficiently depressed, I wonder how they will take this ultimate irony. Few of them have any religious faith, yet they will not relish using this final weapon in their campaign against me— that private, good-natured but fundamentally serious war which lasted all the way from Earth. It amused them to have a Jesuit as chief astrophysicist: Dr. Chandler, for instance, could never get over it (why are medical men such notorious atheists?). Sometimes he would meet me on the observation deck, where the lights are always low so that the stars shine with undiminished glory. He would come up to me in the gloom and stand staring out of the great oval port, while the heavens crawled slowly round us as the ship turned end over end with the residual spin we had never bothered to correct.

"Well, Father," he would say at last. "It goes on forever and forever, and perhaps *Something* made it. But how you can believe that Something has a special interest in us and our miserable little world— that just beats me." Then the argument would start, while the stars and nebulae would swing around us in silent, endless arcs beyond the flawlessly clear plastic of the observation port.

It was, I think, the apparent incongruity of my position which . . . yes, *amused* . . . the crew. In vain I would point to my three papers in the *Astrophysical Journal,* my five in the *Monthly Notices of the Royal Astronomical Society.* I would remind them that our Order has long been famous for its scientific works. We may be few now, but ever since the eighteenth century we have made contributions to astronomy and geophysics out of all proportions to our numbers.

Will my report on the Phoenix Nebula end our thousand years of history? It will end, I fear, much more than that.

I do not know who gave the Nebula its name, which seems to me a very bad one. If it contains a prophecy, it is one which cannot be verified for several thousand million years. Even the word nebula is misleading: this is a far smaller object than those stupendous clouds of mist—the stuff of unborn stars—which are scattered throughout the length of the Milky Way. On the cosmic scale, indeed, the Phoenix Nebula is a tiny thing—a tenuous shell of gas surrounding a single star.

Or what is left of a star . . .

10 The Rubens engraving of Loyola seems to mock me as it hangs 10
there above the spectrophotometer tracings. What would *you*, Father,
have made of this knowledge that has come into my keeping, so far
from the little world that was all the universe you knew? Would your
faith have risen to the challenge, as mine has failed to do?

You gaze into the distance, Father, but I have traveled a distance
beyond any that you could have imagined when you founded our
Order a thousand years ago. No other survey ship has been so far from
Earth: we are at the very frontiers of the explored universe. We set out
to reach the Phoenix Nebula, we succeeded, and we are homeward
bound with our burden of knowledge. I wish I could lift that burden
from my shoulders, but I call to you in vain across the centuries and
the light-years that lie between us.

On the book you are holding the words are plain to read.
AD MAIOREM DEI GLORIAM the message runs, but it is a message I can no longer believe. Would you still believe it, if you could
see what we have found?

We knew, of course, what the Phoenix Nebula was. Every year, in
our galaxy alone, more than a hundred stars explode, blazing for a few
hours or days with thousands of times their normal brilliance before
they sink back into death and obscurity. Such are the ordinary
novae—the commonplace disasters of the universe. I have recorded
the spectrograms and light-curves of dozens, since I started working
at the lunar observatory.

But three or four times in every thousand years occurs something
beside which even a nova pales into total insignificance.

15 When a star becomes a *supernova*, it may for a little while outshine 15
all the massed suns of the galaxy. The Chinese astronomers watched
this happen in 1054 A.D., not knowing what it was they saw. Five
centuries later, in 1572, a supernova blazed in Cassiopeia so brilliantly
that it was visible in the daylight sky. There have been three more in
the thousand years that have passed since then.

Our mission was to visit the remnants of such a catastrophe, to
reconstruct the events that led up to it, and, if possible, to learn its
cause. We came slowly in through the concentric shells of gas that had
been blasted out six thousand years before, yet were expanding still.
They were immensely hot, radiating still with a fierce violet light, but
far too tenuous to do us any damage. When the star had exploded, its
outer layers had been driven upwards with such speed that they had

59

escaped completely from its gravitational field. Now they formed a hollow shell large enough to engulf a thousand solar systems, and at its center burned the tiny, fantastic object which the star had now become—a white dwarf, smaller than the Earth yet weighing a million times as much.

The glowing gas shells were all around us, banishing the normal night of interstellar space. We were flying into the center of a cosmic bomb that had detonated millennia ago and whose incandescent fragments were still hurtling apart. The immense scale of the explosion, and the fact that the debris already covered a volume of space many billions of miles across, robbed the scene of any visible movement. It would take decades before the unaided eye could detect any motion in these tortured wisps and eddies of gas, yet the sense of turbulent expansion was overwhelming.

We had checked our primary drive hours before, and were drifting slowly towards the fierce little star ahead. Once it had been a sun like our own, but it had squandered in a few hours the energy that should have kept it shining for a million years. Now it was a shrunken miser, hoarding its resources as if trying to make amends for its prodigal youth.

No one seriously expected to find planets. If there had been any before the explosion, they would have been boiled into puffs of vapor, and their substance lost in the greater wreckage of the star itself. But we made the automatic search, as always when approaching an unknown sun, and presently we found a single small world circling the star at an immense distance. It must have been the Pluto of this vanished solar system, orbiting on the frontiers of the night. Too far from the central sun ever to have known life, its remoteness had saved it from the fate of all its lost companions.

20   The passing fires had seared its rocks and burnt away the mantle   20 of frozen gas that must have covered it in the days before the disaster. We landed, and we found the Vault.

Its builders had made sure that we should. The monolithic marker that stood above the entrance was now a fused stump, but even the first long-range photographs told us that here was the work of intelligence. A little later we detected the continentwide pattern of radioactivity that had been buried in the rock. Even if the pylon above the Vault had been destroyed, this would have remained, an immovable and all but eternal beacon calling to the stars. Our ship fell towards this gigantic bull's-eye like an arrow into its target.

The pylon must have been a mile high when it was built, but now it looked like a candle that had melted down into a puddle of wax. It took us a week to drill through the fused rock, since we did not have the proper tools for a task like this. We were astronomers, not archaeologists, but we could improvise. Our original program was forgotten: this lonely monument, reared at such labor at the greatest possible distance from the doomed sun, could have only one meaning. A civilization which knew it was about to die had made its last bid for immortality.

It will take us generations to examine all the treasures that were placed in the Vault. *They* had plenty of time to prepare, for their sun must have given its first warnings many years before the final detonation. Everything that they wished to preserve, all the fruits of their genius, they brought here to this distant world in the days before the end, hoping that some other race would find them and that they would not be utterly forgotten.

If only they had had a little more time! They could travel freely enough between the planets of their own sun, but they had not yet learned to cross the interstellar gulfs, and the nearest solar system was a hundred light-years away.

25   Even if they had not been so disturbingly human as their sculp-   25
ture shows, we could not have helped admiring them and grieving for their fate. They left thousands of visual records and the machines for projecting them, together with elaborate pictorial instructions from which it will not be difficult to learn their written language. We have examined many of these records, and brought to life for the first time in six thousand years the warmth and beauty of a civilization which in many ways must have been superior to our own. Perhaps they only showed us the best, and one can hardly blame them. But their worlds were very lovely, and their cities were built with a grace that matches anything of ours. We have watched them at work and play, and listened to their musical speech sounding across the centuries. One scene is still before my eyes—a group of children on a beach of strange blue sand, playing in the waves as children play on Earth.

And sinking into the sea, still warm and friendly and life-giving, is the sun that will soon turn traitor and obliterate all this innocent happiness.

Perhaps if we had not been so far from home and so vulnerable to loneliness, we should not have been so deeply moved. Many of us had seen the ruins of ancient civilizations on other worlds, but they had never affected us so profoundly.

This tragedy was unique. It was one thing for a race to fail and die, as nations and cultures have done on Earth. But to be destroyed so completely in the full flower of its achievement, leaving no survivors—how could that be reconciled with the mercy of God?

My colleagues have asked me that, and I have given what answers I can. Perhaps you could have done better, Father Loyola, but I have found nothing in the *Exercitia Spiritualia* that helps me here. They were not an evil people: I do not know what gods they worshipped, if indeed they worshipped any. But I have looked back at them across the centuries, and have watched while the loveliness they used their last strength to preserve was brought forth again into the light of their shrunken sun.

30   I know the answers that my colleagues will give when they get   30 back to Earth. They will say that the universe has no purpose and no plan, that since a hundred suns explode every year in our galaxy, at this very moment some race is dying in the depths of space. Whether that race has done good or evil during its lifetime will make no difference in the end: there is no divine justice, *for there is no God.*

Yet, of course, what we have seen proves nothing of the sort. Anyone who argues thus is being swayed by emotion, not logic. God has no need to justify His actions to man. He who build the universe can destroy it when He chooses. It is arrogance—it is perilously near blasphemy—for us to say what He may or may not do.

This I could have accepted, hard though it is to look upon whole worlds and peoples thrown into the furnace. But there comes a point when even the deepest faith must falter, and now, as I look at my calculations, I know I have reached that point at last.

We could not tell, before we reached the nebula, how long ago the explosion took place. Now, from the astronomical evidence and the record in the rocks of that one surviving planet, I have been able to date it very exactly. I know in what year the light of this colossal conflagration reached Earth. I know how brilliantly the supernova whose corpse now dwindles behind our speeding ship once shone in terrestrial skies. I know how it must have blazed low in the East before sunrise, like a beacon in that Oriental dawn.

There can be no reasonable doubt: the ancient mystery is solved at last. Yet—O God, there were so many stars you *could* have used.

35   What was the need to give these people to the fire, that the symbol of their passing might shine above Bethlehem? 35

Fun

Wyn Cooper

Wyn Cooper was born in Detroit in 1957. He has taught at Bennington and Marlboro colleges, and now writes full time. He has published three books of poems, most recently Postcards from the Interior. *His poetry has appeared in over 70 magazines and 25 anthologies. He has written songs with Sheryl Crow, David Broza, David Baerwald, and has released two CDs with Madison Smartt Bell. The following poem originally appeared in his first poetry collection,* The Country of Here and Below. *The poem is noteworthy as the basis for the song lyrics of Sheryl Crow's "All I Wanna Do." Compare how the lyrics evolved from the poem. Also, note how the poem's diction and tone lend to its mood and its perspective on life.*

1   "All I want is to have a little fun
    Before I die," says the man next to me
    Out of nowhere, apropos of nothing. He says
    His name's William but I'm sure he's Bill
5   Or Billy, Mac or Buddy; he's plain ugly to me,
    And I wonder if he's ever had fun in his life.

    We are drinking beer at noon on Tuesday,
    In a bar that faces a giant car wash.
    The good people of the world are washing their cars
10 On their lunch hours, hosing and scrubbing
    As best they can in skirts and suits.
    They drive their shiny Datsuns and Buicks
    Back to the phone company, the record store,
    The genetic engineering lab, but not a single one

15 Appears to be having fun like Billy and me.

I like a good beer buzz early in the day,
And Billy likes to peel the labels
From his bottles of Bud and shred them on the bar.
Then he lights every match in an oversized pack,
20 Letting each one burn down to his thick fingers
Before blowing and cursing them out.

A happy couple enters the bar, dangerously close
To one another, like this is a motel,
But they clean up their act when we give them
25 A Look. One quick beer and they're out,
Down the road and in the next state
For all I care, smiling like idiots.
We cover sports and politics and once,
When Billy burns his thumb and lets out a little yelp,
30 The bartender looks up from his want-ads.

Otherwise the bar is ours, and the day and the night
And the car wash too, the matches and the Buds
And the clean and dirty cars, the sun and the moon
And every motel on this highway. It's ours, you hear?
35 And we've got plans, so relax and let us in—
All we want is to have a little fun.

Videotape

Don DeLillo

Don DeLillo (1936–) was born in an Italian-American section of the Bronx, New York. He attended Fordham College where he studied communication arts. He published his first short story in 1960. In 1964 he left his job at an advertising agency to devote himself full-time to writing. His first novel, Americana, *appeared in 1971. Since then, he has written several novels, including* Cosmopolis *(2003),* The Body Artist *(2001),* Underworld *(1997),* Libra *(1988), and* White Noise *(1985), for which he received the National Book Award. The following short story reflects DeLillo's interest in the collective American experience.*

1   It shows a man driving a car. It is the simplest sort of family video. You see a man at the wheel of a medium Dodge.

It is just a kid aiming her camera through the rear window of the family car at the windshield of the car behind her.

You know about families and their video cameras. You know how kids get involved, how the camera shows them that every subject is potentially charged, a million things they never see with the unaided eye. They investigate the meaning of inert objects and dumb pets and they poke fun at family privacy. They learn to see things twice.

It is the kid's own privacy that is being protected here. She is twelve years old and her name is being withheld even though she is neither the victim nor the perpetrator of the crime but only the means of recording it.

5   It shows a man in a sport shirt at the wheel of his car. There is   5
nothing else to see. The car approaches briefly, then falls back.

You know how children with cameras learn to work the exposed
moments that define the family cluster. They break every trust, spy
out the undefended space, catching Mom coming out of the bathroom in her cumbrous robe and turbaned towel, looking bloodless and
plucked. It is not a joke. They will shoot you sitting on the pot if they
can manage a suitable vantage.

The tape has the jostled sort of noneventness that marks the family product. Of course the man in this case is not a member of the
family but a stranger in a car, a random figure, someone who has happened along in the slow lane.

It shows a man in his forties wearing a pale shirt open at the
throat, the image washed by reflections and sunglint, with many jostled moments.

It is not just another video homicide. It is a homicide recorded by
a child who thought she was doing something simple and maybe
halfway clever, shooting some tape of a man in a car.

10   He sees the girl and waves briefly, wagging a hand without taking   10
it off the wheel—an unrelenting reaction that makes you like him.

It is unrelenting footage that rolls on and on. It has an aimless
determination, a persistence that lives outside the subject matter. You
are looking into the mind of home video. It is innocent, it is aimless,
it is determined, it is real.

He is bald up the middle of his head, a nice guy in his forties
whose whole life seems open to the handheld camera.

But there is also an element of suspense. You keep on looking not
because you know something is going to happen—of course you do
know something is going to happen and you do look for that reason
but you might also keep on looking if you came across this footage for
the first time without knowing the outcome. There is a crude power
operating here. You keep on looking because things combine to hold
you fast—a sense of the random, the amateurish, the accidental, the
impending. You don't think of the tape as boring or interesting. It is
crude, it is blunt, it is relentless. It is the jostled part of your mind, the
film that runs through your hotel brain under all the thoughts you
know you're thinking.

The world is lurking in the camera, already framed, waiting for
the boy or girl who will come along and take up the device, learn the

instrument, shooting old Granddad at breakfast, all stroked out so his nostrils gape, the cereal spoon baby-gripped in his pale fist.

15   It shows a man alone in a medium Dodge. It seems to go on for- 15 ever.

There's something about the nature of the tape, the grain of the image, the sputtering black-and-white tones, the starkness—you think this is more real, truer to life than anything around you. The things around you have a rehearsed and layered and cosmetic look. The tape is superreal, or maybe underreal is the way you want to put it. It is what lies at the scraped bottom of all the layers you have added. And this is another reason why you keep on looking. The tape has a searing realness.

It shows him giving an abbreviated wave, stiff-palmed, like a signal flag at a siding.

You know how families make up games. This is just another game in which the child invents the rules as show goes along. She likes the idea of videotaping a man in his car. She has probably never done it before and she sees no reason to vary the format or terminate early or pan to another car. This is her game and she is learning it and playing it at the same time. She feels halfway clever and inventive and maybe slightly intrusive as well, a little bit of brazenness that spices any game.

And you keep on looking. You look because this is the nature of the footage, to make a channeled path through time, to give things a shape and a destiny.

20   Of course if she had panned to another car, the right car at the 20 precise time, she would have caught the gunman as he fired.

The chance quality of the encounter. The victim, the killer, and the child with a camera. Random energies that approach a common point. There's something here that speaks to you directly, saying terrible things about forces beyond your control, lines of intersection that cut through history and logic and every reasonable layer of human expectation.

She wandered into it. The girl got lost and wandered clear-eyed into horror. This is a children's story about straying too far from home. But it isn't the family car that serves as the instrument of the child's curiosity, her inclination to explore. It is the camera that puts her in the tale.

You know about holidays and family celebrations and how somebody shows up with a camcorder and the relatives stand around and barely react because they're numbingly accustomed to the process of being taped and decked and shown on the VCR with the coffee and cake.

He is hit soon after. If you've seen the tape many times you know from the handwave exactly when he will be hit. It is something, naturally, that you wait for. You say to your wife, if you're at home and she is there, Now here is where he gets it. You say, Janet, hurry up, this is where it happens.

25   Now here is where he gets it. You see him jolted, sort of wire shocked—then he seizes up and falls toward the door or maybe leans or slides into the door is the proper way to put it. It is awful and unremarkable at the same time. The car stays in the slow lane. It approaches briefly, then falls back.

You don't usually call your wife over to the TV set. She has her programs, you have yours. But there's a certain urgency here. You want her to see how it looks. The tape has been running forever and now the thing is finally going to happen and you want her to be here when he's shot.

Here it comes, all right. He is shot, head-shot, and the camera reacts, the child reacts—there is a jostling movement but she keeps on taping, there is a sympathetic response, a nerve response, her heart is beating faster but she keeps the camera trained on the subject as he slides into the door and even as you see him die you're thinking of the girl. At some level the girl has to be present here, watching what you're watching, unprepared—the girl is seeing this cold and you have to marvel at the fact that she keeps the tape rolling.

It shows something awful and unaccompanied. You want your wife to see it because it is real this time, not fancy movie violence— the realness beneath the layers of cosmetic perception. Hurry up, Janet, here it comes. He dies so fast. There is no accompaniment of any kind. It is very stripped. You want to tell her it is realer than real but then she will ask what that means.

The way the camera reacts to the gunshot—a startle reaction that brings pity and terror into the frame, the girl's own shock, the girl's identification with the victim.

30   You don't see the blood, which is trickling behind his ear, and down the back of his neck. The way his head is twisting away from the door, the twist of the head gives you only a partial profile and it's the wrong side, it's not the side where he was hit.

And maybe you're being a little aggressive here, practically forcing your wife to watch. Why? What are you telling her? Are you making a little statement? Like I'm going to ruin your day out of ordinary spite. Or a big statement? Like this is the risk of existing. Either way you're rubbing her face in this tape and you don't know why.

It shows the car drifting toward the guardrail and then there's a jostling sense of two other lanes and part of another car, a split-second blur, and the tape ends here, either because the girl stopped shooting or because some central authority, the police or the district attorney or the TV station, decided there was nothing else you had to see.

This is either the tenth or eleventh homicide committed by the Texas Highway Killer. The number is uncertain because the police believe that one of the shootings may have been a copycat crime.

And there is something about videotape, isn't there, and this particular kind of serial crime? This is a crime designed for random taping and immediate playing. You sit there and wonder if this kind of crime became more possible when the means of taping and playing an event—playing it immediately after the taping—became part of the culture. The principal doesn't necessarily commit the sequence of crimes in order to see them taped and played. He commits the crimes as if they were a form of taped-and-played event. The crimes are inseparable from the idea of taping and playing. You sit there thinking that this is a crime that has found its medium, or vice versa—cheap mass production, the sequence of repeated images and victims, stark and glary and more or less unremarkable.

35   It shows very little in the end. It is a famous murder because it is   35
on tape and because the murderer has done it many times and because the crime was recorded by a child. So the child is involved, the Video Kid as she is sometimes called because they have to call her something. The tape is famous and so is she. She is famous in the modern manner of people whose names are strategically withheld. They are famous without names or faces, spirits living apart from their bodies, the victims and witnesses, the underage criminals, out there somewhere at the edges of perception.

Seeing someone at the moment he dies, dying unexpectedly. This is the reason alone to stay fixed on the screen. It is instructional, watching a man shot dead as he drives along on a sunny day. It demonstrates an elemental truth, that every breath you take has two possible endings. And that's another thing. There's a joke locked away here, a note of cruel slapstick that you are willing to appreciate even if it makes you feel a little guilty. Maybe the victim's a chump, a sort of silent-movie dupe, classically unlucky. He had it coming in a sense, for letting himself be caught on camera. Because once the tape starts rolling it can only end one way. This is what the context requires.

You don't want Janet to give you any crap about it's on all the time, they show it a thousand times a day. They show it because it exists, because they have to show it, because this is why they're out there, to provide our entertainment.

The more you watch the tape, the deader and colder and more relentless it becomes. The tape sucks the air right out of your chest but you watch it every time.

Battle Royal

Ralph Ellison

Ralph Waldo Ellison was born in Oklahoma City in 1914 and died of cancer in 1994. He developed a youthful interest in music and accepted a scholarship to Tuskegee Institute in Alabama to pursue it. There he developed an interest in writing, and after moving to New York City in 1936, joined the Federal Writers' Project. His first novel, Invisible Man *(1952), was an international success and won him won the National Book Award. This excerpt from* Invisible Man *illustrates Ellison's elegant prose style and the disciplined storytelling style that enables his reader to experience firsthand the naiveté and suffering of a young man who is being tortured by white racists.*

1   It goes a long way back, some twenty years. All my life I had been   1
looking for something, and everywhere I turned someone tried to
tell me what it was. I accepted their answers too, though they were
often in contradiction and even self-contradictory. I was naive. I was
looking for myself and asking everyone except myself questions which
I, and only I, could answer. It took me a long time and much painful
boomeranging of my expectations to achieve a realization everyone
else appears to have been born with: That I am nobody but myself.
But first I had to discover that I am an invisible man!

And yet I am no freak of nature, nor of history. I was in the cards,
other things having been equal (or unequal) eighty-five years ago. I am
not ashamed of my grandparents for having been slaves. I am only
ashamed of myself for having at one time been ashamed. About
eighty-five years ago they were told that they were free, united with
others of our country in everything pertaining to the common good,
and, in everything social, separate like the fingers of the hand. And

they believed it. They exulted in it. They stayed in their place, worked hard, and brought up my father to do the same. But my grandfather is the one. He was an odd old guy, my grandfather, and I am told I take after him. It was he who caused the trouble. On his deathbed he called my father to him and said, "Son, after I'm gone I want you to keep up the good fight. I never told you, but our life is a war and I have been a traitor all my born days, a spy in the enemy's country ever since I give up my gun back in the Reconstruction. Live with your head in the lion's mouth. I want you to overcome 'em with yeses, undermine 'em with grins, agree 'em to death and destruction, let 'em swoller you till they vomit or bust wide open." They thought the old man had gone out of his mind. He had been the meekest of men. The younger children were rushed from the room, the shades drawn and the flame of the lamp turned so low that it sputtered on the wick like the old man's breathing. "Learn it to the younguns," he whispered fiercely; then he died.

But my folks were more alarmed over his last words than over his dying. It was as though he had not died at all, his words caused so much anxiety. I was warned emphatically to forget what he had said and, indeed, this is the first time it has been mentioned outside the family circle. It had a tremendous effect upon me, however, I could never be sure of what he meant. Grandfather had been a quiet old man who never made any trouble, yet on his deathbed he had called himself a traitor and a spy, and he had spoken of his meekness as a dangerous activity. It became a constant puzzle which lay unanswered in the back of my mind. And whenever things went well for me I remembered my grandfather and felt guilty and uncomfortable. It was as though I was carrying out his advice in spite of myself. And to make it worse, everyone loved me for it. I was praised by the most lily-white men of the town. I was considered an example of desirable conduct— just as my grandfather had been. And what puzzled me was that the old man had defined it as *treachery*. When I was praised for my conduct I felt a guilt that in some way I was doing something that was really against the wishes of the white folks, that if they had understood they would have desired me to act just the opposite, that I should have been sulky and mean, and that that really would have been what they wanted, even though they were fooled and thought they wanted me to act as I did. It made me afraid that some day they would look upon me as a traitor and I would be lost. Still I was more afraid to act any other way because they didn't like that at all. The old man's words were like a curse. On my graduation day I delivered an oration in which I showed that humility was the secret, indeed, the very essence of progress. (Not that I believed this—how could I, remembering my grandfather?—I only believed that it worked.) It was a great success. Everyone praised me and I was invited to give the speech at a gathering of the town's leading white citizens. It was a triumph for our whole community.

It was in the main ballroom of the leading hotel. When I got there I discovered that it was on the occasion of a smoker, and I was told that since I was to be there anyway I might as well take part in the battle royal to be fought by some of my schoolmates as part of the entertainment. The battle royal came first.

5   All of the town's big shots were there in their tuxedoes, wolfing down the buffet foods, drinking beer and whiskey and smoking black cigars. It was a large room with a high ceiling. Chairs were arranged in neat rows around three sides of a portable boxing ring. The fourth side was clear, revealing a gleaming space of polished floor. I had some misgivings over the battle royal, by the way. Not from a distaste for fighting, but because I didn't care too much for the other fellows who were to take part. They were tough guys who seemed to have no grandfather's curse worrying their minds. No one could mistake their toughness. And besides, I suspected that fighting a battle royal might detract from the dignity of my speech. In those pre-invisible days I visualized myself as a potential Booker T. Washington. But the other fellows didn't care too much for me either, and there were nine of them. I felt superior to them in my way, and I didn't like the manner in which we were all crowded together into the servants' elevator. Nor did they like my being there. In fact, as the warmly lighted floors flashed past the elevator we had words over the fact that I, by taking part in the fight, had knocked one of their friends out of a night's work.

We were led out of the elevator through a rococo hall into an anteroom and told to get into our fighting togs. Each of us was issued a pair of boxing gloves and ushered out into the big mirrored hall, which we entered looking cautiously about us and whispering, lest we might accidentally be heard above the noise of the room. It was foggy with cigar smoke. And already the whiskey was taking effect. I was shocked to see some of the most important men of the town quite

74

tipsy. They were all there—bankers, lawyers, judges, doctors, fire chiefs, teachers, merchants. Even one of the more fashionable pastors. Something we could not see was going on up front. A clarinet was vibrating sensuously and the men were standing up and moving eagerly forward. We were a small tight group, clustered together, our bare upper bodies touching and shining with anticipatory sweat; while up front the big shots were becoming increasingly excited over something we still could not see. Suddenly I heard the school superintendent, who had told me to come, yell, "Bring up the shines, gentlemen! Bring up the little shines!"

We were rushed up to the front of the ballroom, where it smelled even more strongly of tobacco and whiskey. Then we were pushed into place. I almost wet my pants. A sea of faces, some hostile, some amused, ringed around us, and in the center, facing us, stood a magnificent blonde—stark naked. There was dead silence. I felt a blast of cold air chill me. I tried to back away, but they were behind me and around me. Some of the boys stood with lowered heads, trembling. I felt a wave of irrational guilt and fear. My teeth chattered, my skin turned to goose flesh, my knees knocked. Yet I was strongly attracted and looked in spite of myself. Had the price of looking been blindness, I would have looked. The hair was yellow like that of a circus kewpie doll, the face heavily powdered and rouged, as though to form an abstract mask, the eyes hollow and smeared a cool blue, the color of a baboon's butt. I felt a desire to spit upon her as my eyes brushed slowly over her body. Her breasts were firm and round as the domes of East Indian temples, and I stood so close as to see the fine skin texture and beads of pearly perspiration glistening like dew around the pink and erected buds of her nipples. I wanted at one and the same time to run from the room, to sink through the floor, or go to her and cover her from my eyes and the eyes of the others with my body; to feel the soft thighs, to caress her and destroy her, to love her and murder her, to hide from her, and yet to stroke where below the small American flag tattooed upon her belly her thighs formed a capital V. I had a notion that of all in the room she saw only me with her impersonal eyes.

And then she began to dance, a slow sensuous movement; the smoke of a hundred cigars clinging to her like the thinnest of veils. She seemed like a fair bird-girl girdled in veils calling to me from the angry surface of some gray and threatening sea. I was transported.

Then I became aware of the clarinet playing and the big shots yelling at us. Some threatened us if we looked and others if we did not. On my right I saw one boy faint. And now a man grabbed a silver pitcher from a table and stepped close as he dashed ice water upon him and stood him up and forced two of us to support him as his head hung and moans issued from his thick bluish lips. Another boy began to plead to go home. He was the largest of the group, wearing dark red fighting trunks much too small to conceal the erection which projected from him as though in answer to the insinuating low-registered moaning of the clarinet. He tried to hide himself with his boxing gloves.

And all the while the blonde continued dancing, smiling faintly at the big shots who watched her with fascination, and faintly smiling at our fear. I noticed a certain merchant who followed her hungrily, his lips loose and drooling. He was a large man who wore diamond studs in a shirtfront which swelled with the ample paunch underneath, and each time the blonde swayed her undulating hips he ran his hand through the thin hair of his bald head and, with his arms upheld, his posture clumsy like that of an intoxicated panda, wound his belly in a slow and obscene grind. This creature was completely hypnotized. The music had quickened. As the dancer flung herself about with a detached expression on her face, the men began reaching out to touch her. I could see their beefy fingers sink into the soft flesh. Some of the others tried to stop them and she began to move around the floor in graceful circles, as they gave chase, slipping and sliding over the polished floor. It was mad. Chairs went crashing, drinks were spilt, as they ran laughing and howling after her. They caught her just as she reached a door, raised her from the floor, and tossed her as college boys are tossed at a hazing, and above her red, fixed-smiling lips I saw the terror and disgust in her eyes, almost like my own terror and that which I saw in some of the other boys. As I watched, they tossed her twice and her soft breasts seemed to flatten against the air and her legs flung wildly as she spun. Some of the sober ones helped her to escape. And I started off the floor, heading for the anteroom with the rest of the boys.

10 Some were still crying and in hysteria. But as we tried to leave we 10 were stopped and ordered to get into the ring. There was nothing to do but what we were told. All ten of us climbed under the ropes and allowed ourselves to be blindfolded with broad bands of white cloth.

One of the men seemed to feel a bit sympathetic and tried to cheer us up as we stood with our backs against the ropes. Some of us tried to grin. "See that boy over there?" one of the men said. "I want you to run across at the bell and give it to him right in the belly. If you don't get him, I'm going to get you. I don't like his looks." Each of us was told the same. The blindfolds were put on. Yet even then I had been going over my speech. In my mind each word was as bright as flame. I felt the cloth pressed into place, and frowned so that it would be loosened when I relaxed.

But now I felt a sudden fit of blind terror. I was unused to darkness. It was as though I had suddenly found myself in a dark room filled with poisonous cottonmouths. I could hear the bleary voices yelling insistently for the battle royal to begin.

"Get going in there!"

"Let me at that big nigger!"

I strained to pick up the school superintendent's voice, as though to squeeze some security out of that slightly more familiar sound.

"Let me at those black sonsabitches!" someone yelled.

"No, Jackson, no!" another voice yelled. "Here, somebody, help me hold Jack."

"I want to get at that ginger-colored nigger. Tear him limb from limb," the first voice yelled.

I stood against the ropes trembling. For in those days I was what they called ginger-colored, and he sounded as though he might crunch me between his teeth like a crisp ginger cookie.

Quite a struggle was going on. Chairs were being kicked about and I could hear voices grunting as with a terrific effort. I wanted to see, to see more desperately than ever before. But the blindfold was tight as a thick skin-puckering scab and when I raised my gloved hands to push the layers of white aside a voice yelled, "Oh, no you don't, black bastard! Leave that alone!"

"Ring the bell before Jackson kills him a coon!" someone boomed in the sudden silence. And I heard the bell clang and the sound of the feet scuffling forward.

A glove smacked against my head. I pivoted, striking out stiffly as someone went past, and felt the jar ripple along the length of my arm to my shoulder. Then it seemed as though all nine boys had turned upon me at once. Blows pounded me from all sides while I struck out as best I could. So many blows landed upon me that I wondered if I were not the only blindfolded fighter in the ring, or if the man called Jackson hadn't succeeded in getting me after all.

Blindfolded, I could no longer control my motions. I had no dignity. I stumbled about like a baby or a drunken man. The smoke had become thicker and with each new blow it seemed to sear and further restrict my lungs. My saliva became like hot bitter glue. A glove connected with my head, filling my mouth with warm blood. It was everywhere. I could not tell if the moisture I felt upon my body was sweat or blood. A blow landed hard against the nape of my neck. I felt myself going over, my head hitting the floor. Streaks of blue light filled the black world behind the blindfold. I lay prone, pretending that I was knocked out, but felt myself seized by hands and yanked to my feet. "Get going, black boy! Mix it up!" My arms were like lead, my head smarting from blows. I managed to feel my way to the ropes and held on, trying to catch my breath. A glove landed in my mid-section and I went over again, feeling as though the smoke had become a knife jabbed into my guts. Pushed this way and that by the legs milling around me, I finally pulled erect and discovered that I could see the black, sweat-washed forms weaving in the smoky-blue atmosphere like drunken dancers weaving to the rapid drum-like thuds of blows.

Everyone fought hysterically. It was complete anarchy. Everybody fought everybody else. No group fought together for long. Two, three, four, fought one, then turned to fight each other, were themselves attacked. Blows landed below the belt and in the kidney, with the gloves open as well as closed, and with my eye partly opened now there was not so much terror. I moved carefully, avoiding blows, although not too many to attract attention, fighting from group to group. The boys groped about like blind, cautious crabs crouching to protect their mid-sections, their heads pulled in short against their shoulders, their arms stretched nervously before them, with their fists testing the smoke-filled air like the knobbed feelers of hypersensitive snails. In one corner I glimpsed a boy violently punching the air and heard him scream in pain as he smashed his hand against a ring post. For a second I saw him bent over holding his hand, then going down as a blow caught his unprotected head. I played one group against the other, slipping in and throwing a punch then stepping out of range while pushing the others into the melee to take the blows blindly aimed at me. The smoke was agonizing and there were no rounds, no bells at three minute intervals to relieve our exhaustion. The room spun round me, a swirl of lights, smoke, sweating bodies sourrounded by tense white faces. I bled from both nose and mouth, the blood spattering upon my chest.

The men kept yelling, "Slug him, black boy! Knock his guts out!"

"Uppercut him! Kill him! Kill that big boy!"

Taking a fake fall, I saw a boy going down heavily beside me as though we were felled by a single blow, saw a sneaker-clad foot shot into his groin as the two who had knocked him down stumbled upon him. I rolled out of range, feeling a twinge of nausea.

The harder we fought the more threatening the men became. And yet, I had begun to worry about my speech again. How would it go? Would they recognize my ability? What would they give me?

I was fighting automatically when suddenly I noticed that one after another of the boys was leaving the ring. I was surprised, filled with panic, as though I had been left alone with an unknown danger. Then I understood. The boys had arranged it among themselves. It was the custom for the two men left in the ring to slug it out for the winner's prize. I discovered this too late. When the bell sounded two men in tuxedoes leaped into the ring and removed the blindfold. I found myself facing Tatlock, the biggest of the gang. I felt sick at my stomach. Hardly had the bell stopped ringing in my ears than it clanged again and I saw him moving swiftly toward me. Thinking of nothing else to do I hit him smash on the nose. He kept coming, bringing the rank sharp violence of stale sweat. His face was a black blank of a face, only his eyes alive—with hate of me and aglow with a feverish terror from what had happened to us all. I became anxious. I wanted to deliver my speech and he came at me as though he meant to beat it out of me. I smashed him again and again, taking his blows as they came. Then on a sudden impulse I struck him lightly and as we clinched, I whispered, "Fake like I knocked you out, you can have the prize."

"I'll break your behind," he whispered hoarsely.

"For *them*?"

"For *me*, sonofabitch!"

They were yelling for us to break it up and Tatlock spun me half around with a blow, and as a joggled camera sweeps in a reefing scene, I saw the howling red faces crouching tense beneath the cloud of blue-gray smoke. For a moment the world wavered, unraveled, flowed, then my head cleared and Tatlock bounced before me. The

25

30

fluttering shadow before my eyes was his jabbing left hand. Then falling forward, my head against his damp shoulder, I whispered, "I'll make it five dollars more."

"Go to hell!"

35 But his muscles relaxed a trifle beneath my pressure and I breathed, "Seven?"

"Give it to your ma," he said, ripping me beneath the heart.

And while I still held him I butted him and moved away. I felt myself bombarded with punches. I fought back with hopeless desperation. I wanted to deliver my speech more than anything else in the world, because I felt that only these men could judge truly my ability, and now this stupid clown was ruining my chances. I began fighting carefully now, moving in to punch him and out again with my greater speed. A lucky blow to his chin and I had him going too—until I heard a loud voice yell, "I got my money on the big boy."

Hearing this, I almost dropped my guard. I was confused: Should I try to win against the voice out there? Would not this go against my speech, and was not this a moment for humility, for nonresistance? A blow to my head as I danced about sent my right eye popping like a jack-in-the-box and settled my dilemma. The room went red as I fell. It was a dream fall, my body languid and fastidious as to where to land, until the floor became impatient and smashed up to meet me. A moment later I came to. An hypnotic vice said FIVE emphatically. And I lay there, hazily watching a dark red spot of my own blood shaping itself into a butterfly, glistening and soaking into the soiled gray world of the canvas.

When the voice drawled TEN I was lifted up and dragged to a chair. I sat dazed. My eye pained and swelled with each throb of my pounding heart and I wondered if now I would be allowed to speak. I was wringing wet, my mouth still bleeding. We were grouped along the wall now. The other boys ignored me as they congratulated Tatlock and speculated as to how much they would be paid. One boy whimpered over his smashed hand. Looking up front, I saw attendants in white jackets rolling the portable ring away and placing a small square rug in the vacant space surrounded by chairs. Perhaps, I thought, I will stand on the rug to deliver my speech.

40 Then the M. C. called to us, "Come on up here boys and get your money."

We ran forward to where the men laughed and talked in their chairs, waiting. Everyone seemed friendly now.

"There it is on the rug," the man said. I saw the rug covered with coins of all dimensions and a few crumpled bills. But what excited me, scattered here and there, were the gold pieces.

"Boys, it's all yours," the man said. "You get all you grab."

"That's right, Sambo," a blond man said, winking at me confidentially.

45 I trembled with excitement, forgetting my pain. I would get the gold and the bills, I thought. I would use both hands. I would throw my body against the boys nearest me to block them from the gold.

"Get down on the rug now," the man commanded, "and don't anyone touch it until I give the signal."

"This ought to be good," I heard.

As told, we got around the square rug on our knees. Slowly the man raised his freckled hand as we followed it upward with our eyes.

I heard, "These niggers look like they're about to pray!"

50 Then, "Ready," the man said, "Go!"

I lunged for a yellow coin lying on the blue design of the carpet, touching it and sending a surprised shriek to join those rising around me. I tried frantically to remove my hand but could not let go. A hot, violent force tore through my body, shaking me like a wet rage. The rug was electrified. The hair bristled up on my head as I shook myself free. My muscles jumped, my nerves jangled, writhed. But I saw that this was not stopping the other boys. Laughing in fear and embarrassment, some were holding back and scooping up the coins knocked off by the painful contortions of the others. The men roared above us as we struggled.

"Pick it up, goddamnit, pick it up!" someone called like a bass-voiced parrot. "Go on, get it!"

I crawled rapidly around the floor, picking up the coins, trying to avoid the coppers and to get greenbacks and the gold. Ignoring the shock by laughing, as I brushed the coins off quickly, I discovered that I could contain the electricity—a contradiction, but it works. Then the men began to push us onto the rug. Laughing embarrassedly, we struggled out of their hands and kept after the coins. We were all wet and slippery and hard to hold. Suddenly I saw a boy lifted into the air, glistening with sweat like a circus seal, and dropped, his wet back landing flush upon the charged rug, heard him yell and saw him literally dance upon his back, his elbows beating a frenzied tattoo upon the floor, his muscles twitching like the flesh of a horse stung by many flies. When he finally rolled off, his face was gray and no one stopped him when he ran from the floor amid booming laughter.

"Get the money," the M. C. called. "That's good hard American cash!"

55   And we snatched and grabbed, snatched and grabbed. I was care-   55 ful not to come too close to the rug now, and when I felt the hot whiskey breath descend upon me like a cloud of foul air I reached out and grabbed the leg of a chair. It was occupied and I held on desperately.

"Leggo, nigger! Leggo!"

The huge face wavered down to mine as he tried to push me free. But my body was slippery and he was too drunk. It was Mr. Colcord, who owned a chain of movie houses and "entertainment palaces." Each time he grabbed me I slipped out of his hands. It became a real struggle. I feared the rug more than I did the drunk, so I held on, surprising myself for a moment by trying to topple *him* upon the rug. It was such an enormous idea that I found myself actually carrying it out. I tried not to be obvious, yet when I grabbed his leg, trying to tumble him out of the chair, he raised up roaring with laughter, and, looking at me with soberness dead in the eye, kicked me viciously in the chest. The chair leg flew out of my hand and I felt myself going and rolled. It was as though I had rolled through a bed of hot coals. It seemed a whole century would pass before I would roll free, a century in which I was seared through the deepest levels of my body to the fearful breath within me and the breath seared and heated to the point of explosion. It'll all be over in a flash, I thought as I rolled clear. It'll all be over in a flash.

But not yet, the men on the other side were waiting, red faces swollen as though from apoplexy as they bent forward in their chairs. Seeing their fingers coming toward me, I rolled away as a fumbled football rolls off the receiver's fingertips, back into the coals. That time I luckily sent the rug sliding out of place and heard the coins ringing against the floor and the boys scuffling to pick them up and the M.C. calling, "All right, boys that's all. Go get dressed and get your money."

I was limp as a dish rag. My back felt as though it had been beaten with wires.

60 When we had dressed the M.C. came in and gave us each five dollars, except Tatlock, who got ten for being last in the ring. Then he told us to leave. I was not to get a chance to deliver my speech, I thought. I was going out into the dim alley in despair when I was stopped and told to go back. I returned to the ballroom, where the men were pushing back their chairs and gathering in groups to talk.

The M.C. knocked on a table for quiet. "Gentlemen," he said, "we almost forgot about an important part of the program. A most serious part, gentlemen. This boy was brought here to deliver a speech which he made at his graduation yesterday . . ."

"Bravo! "

"I'm told that he is the smartest boy we've got out there in Greenwood. I'm told that he knows more big words than a pocket-sized dictionary."

Much applause and laughter.

"So now, gentlemen, I want you to give him your attention."

65 There was still laughter as I faced them, my mouth dry, my eye throbbing. I began slowly, but evidently my throat was tense, because they began shouting, "Louder! Louder!"

"We of the younger generation extol the wisdom of that great leader and educator," I shouted, "who first spoke these flaming words of wisdom: 'A ship lost at sea for many days suddenly sighted a friendly vessel. From the mast of the unfortunate vessel was seen a signal: "Water, water; we die of thirst!" The answer from the friendly vessel came back: "Cast down your bucket where you are." The captain of the distressed vessel, at last heeding the injunction, cast down his bucket, and it came up fill of fresh sparkling water from the mouth of the Amazon River.' And like him I say, and in his words, 'To those of my race who depend upon bettering their condition in a foreign land, or who underestimate the importance of cultivating friendly relations with the Southern white man, who is his next-door neighbor, I would say: "Cast down your bucket where you are"—cast it down in making friends in every manly way of the people of all races by whom we are surrounded . . ."

I spoke automatically and with such fervor that I did not realize that the men were still talking and laughing until my dry mouth, filling up with blood from the cut, almost strangled me. I coughed, wanting to stop and go to one of the tall brass, sand-filled spittoons to relieve myself, but a few of the men, especially the superintendent, were listening and I was afraid. So I gulped it down, blood, saliva and all, and continued. (What powers of endurance I had during those days! What enthusiasm! What a belief in the rightness of things!) I spoke even louder in spite of the pain. But still they talked and still they laughed, as though deaf with cotton in dirty ears. So I spoke with greater emotional emphasis. I closed my ears and swallowed blood until I was nauseated. The speech seemed a hundred times as long as before, but I could not leave out a single word. All had to be said, each memorized nuance considered, rendered. Nor was that all. Whenever I uttered a word of three syllables a group of voices would yell for me to repeat it. I used the phrase "social responsibility" and they yelled:

"What's that word you say, boy?"

"Social responsibility," I said.

"What?"

"Social. . . ."

"Louder."

". . . responsibility."

"More!"

"Respon—"

"Repeat!"

"—sibility."

The room filled with the uproar of laughter until, no doubt, distracted by having to gulp down my blood, I made a mistake and yelled a phrase I had often seen denounced in newspaper editorials, heard debated in private.

"Social . . ."

"Louder."

"What?" they yelled.

". . . equality—"

The laughter hung smokelike in the sudden stillness. I opened my eyes, puzzled. Sounds of displeasure filled the room. The M.C. rushed forward. They shouted hostile phrases at me. But I did not understand.

A small dry mustached man in the front row blared out, "Say that slowly, son!"

"What, sir?"

"What you just said!"

"Social responsibility, sir," I said.

"You weren't being smart, were you, boy?" he said, not unkindly.

"No, sir!"

"You sure that about 'equality' was a mistake?"

90 "Oh, yes sir," I said. "I was swallowing blood." 90

"Well, you had better speak more slowly so we can understand. We mean to do right by you, but you've got to know your place at all times. All right, now, go on with your speech."

I was afraid. I wanted to leave but I wanted also to speak and I was afraid they'd snatch me down.

"Thank you, sir," I said, beginning where I had left off, and having them ignore me as before.

Yet when I finished there was a thunderous applause. I was surprised to see the superintendent come forth with a package wrapped in white tissue paper, and, gesturing for quiet, address the men.

95 "Gentlemen, you see that I did not overpraise this boy. He makes 95 a good speech and some day he'll lead his people in the proper paths. And I don't have to tell you that that is important in these days and times. This is a good, smart boy, and so to encourage him in the right direction, in the name of the Board of Education I wish to present him a prize in the form of this . . ."

He paused, removing the tissue paper and revealing a gleaming calfskin brief case.

". . . in the form of this first-class article from Shad Whitmore's shop."

"Boy," he said, addressing me, "take this prize and keep it well. Consider it a badge of office. Prize it. Keep developing as you are and some day it will be filled with important papers that will help shape the destiny of your people."

I was so moved that I could hardly express my thanks. A rope of bloody saliva forming a shape like an undiscovered continent drooled upon the leather and I wiped it quickly away. I felt an importance that I had never dreamed.

100 "Open it and see what's inside," I was told. 100

My fingers a-tremble, I complied, smelling the fresh leather and finding an official-looking document inside. It was a scholarship to the state college for Negroes. My eyes filled with tears and I ran awkwardly off the floor.

I was overjoyed; I did not even mind when I discovered that the gold pieces I had scrambled for were brass pocket tokens advertising a certain make of automobile.

When I reached home everyone was excited. Next day the neighbors came to congratulate me. I even felt safe from grandfather, whose deathbed curse usually spoiled my triumphs. I stood beneath his photograph with my brief case in hand and smiled triumphantly into his stolid black peasant's face. It was a face that fascinated me. The eyes seemed to follow everywhere I went.

That night I dreamed I was at a circus with him and that he refused to laugh at the clowns no matter what they did. Then later he told me to open my brief case and read what was inside and I did, finding an official envelope stamped with the state seal; and inside the envelope, I found another and another, endlessly, and I thought I would fall of weariness. "Them's years," he said. "Now open that one." And I did and in it I found an engraved document containing a short message in letters of gold. "Read it," my grandfather said. "Out loud!"

105   "To Whom It May Concern," I intoned. "Keep This Nigger-Boy 105 Running."

I awoke with the old man's laughter ringing in my ears.

(It was a dream I was to remember and dream again for many years after. But at that time I had no insight into its meaning. First I had to attend college.)

Birches

Robert Frost

Robert Frost (1874-1963), the American poet everyone knows, was born in San Francisco, studied at Dartmouth and Harvard, worked in a mill, taught school, and farmed in New Hampshire before his first volume of poems was published. Having achieved prominence in the United States by 1915, he taught at many colleges and universities as well as at the famous Bread Loaf Writer's Conference. He won the Pulitzer four times, had a mountain in Vermont named after him, and read at John F. Kennedy's inauguration. He aspired to write a few poems it would be hard to get rid of, an ambition he achieved in "Stopping by Woods on a Snowy Evening," "The Death of the Hired Man," and "Birches," among others. "Birches" is typical of Frost's work in its rural themes and philosophical reflection.

1   When I see birches bend to left and right   1
     Across the lines of straighter darker trees,
     I like to think some boy's been swinging them.
     But swinging doesn't bend them down to stay
5   As ice storms do. Often you must have seen them   5
     Loaded with ice a sunny winter morning
     After a rain. They click upon themselves
     As the breeze rises, and turn many-colored
     As the stir cracks and crazes their enamel.
10   Soon the sun's warmth makes them shed crystal shells   10
     Shattering and avalanching on the snow crust—
     Such heaps of broken glass to sweep away
     You'd think the inner dome of heaven had fallen.
     They are dragged to the withered bracken by the load,

15 And they seem not to break; though once they are bowed
So low for long, they never right themselves:
You may see their trunks arching in the woods
Years afterwards, trailing their leaves on the ground
Like girls on hands and knees that throw their hair
20 Before them over their heads to dry in the sun.
But I was going to say when Truth broke in
With all her matter of fact about the ice storm,
I should prefer to have some boy bend them
As he went out and in to fetch the cows—
25 Some boy too far from town to learn baseball,
Whose only play was what he found himself,
Summer or winter, and could play alone.
One by one he subdued his father's trees
By riding them down over and over again
30 Until he took the stiffness out of them,
And not one but hung limp, not one was left
For him to conquer. He learned all there was
To learn about not launching out too soon
And so not carrying the tree away
35 Clear to the ground. He always kept his poise
To the top branches, climbing carefully
With the same pains you use to fill a cup
Up to the brim, and even above the brim.
Then he flung outward, feet first, with a swish,
40 Kicking his way down through the air to the ground.
So was I once myself a swinger of birches.
And so I dream of going back to be.
It's when I'm weary of considerations,
And life is too much like a pathless wood
45 Where your face burns and tickles with the cobwebs
Broken across it, and one eye is weeping
From a twig's having lashed across it open.
I'd like to get away from earth awhile
And then come back to it and begin over.
50 May no fate willfully misunderstand me
And half grant what I wish and snatch me away
Not to return. Earth's the right place for love:
I don't know where it's likely to go better.

I'd like to go by climbing a birch tree,
55 And climb black branches up a snow-white trunk   55
Toward heaven, till the tree could bear no more,
But dipped its top and set me down again.
That would be good both going and coming back.
One could do worse than be a swinger of birches.

Mending Wall

Robert Frost

Robert Frost (1874–1963), the American poet everyone knows, was born in San Fransisco, studied at Dartmouth and Harvard, worked in a mill, taught school, and farmed in New Hamphshire before his first volume of poems was published. Having achieved prominence in the United States by 1915, he taught at many colleges and universities as well as at the famous Bread Loaf Writer's Conference. He won the Pulitzer four times, had a mountain in Vermont named after him, and read at John F. Kennedy's inaguration. He aspired to write a few poems it would be hard to get rid of, an ambition he achieved in "Stopping by Woods on a Snowy Evening," "The Death of the Hired Man," and "Birches," among others. This 1914 poem recounts the annual spring ritual of neighbors repairing a stone wall, prompting the poet to wonder why people believe that good fences make good neighbors.

1   Something there is that doesn't love a wall,
That sends the frozen-ground-swell under it,
And spills the upper boulders in the sun;
And makes gaps even two can pass abreast.
5   The work of hunters is another thing:
I have come after them and made repair
Where they have left not one stone on a stone,
But they would have the rabbit out of hiding,
To please the yelping dogs. The gaps I mean,
10   No one has seen them made or heard them made,
But at spring mending-time we find them there.
I let my neighbor know beyond the hill;

And on a day we meet to walk the line
And set the wall between us once again.
We keep the wall between us as we go.
To each the boulders that have fallen to each.
And some are loaves and some so nearly balls
We have to use a spell to make them balance:
"Stay where you are until our backs are turned!"
We wear our fingers rough with handling them.
Oh, just another kind of outdoor game,
One on a side. It comes to little more:
There where it is we do not need the wall:
He is all pine and I am apple orchard.
My apple trees will never get across
And eat the cones under his pines, I tell him.
He only says, "Good fences make good neighbors."
Spring is the mischief in me, and I wonder
If I could put a notion in his head:
"*Why* do they make good neighbors? Isn't it
Where there are cows? But here there are no cows.
Before I built a wall I'd ask to know
What I was walling in or walling out,
And to whom I was like to give offense.
Something there is that doesn't love a wall,
That wants it down." I could say "Elves" to him,
But it's not elves exactly, and I'd rather
He said it for himself. I see him there
Bringing a stone grasped firmly by the top
In each hand, like an old-stone savage armed.
He moves in darkness as it seems to me,
Not of woods only and the shade of trees.
He will not go behind his father's saying,
And he likes having thought of it so well
He says again, "Good fences make good neighbors."

A Rose for Emily

William Faulkner

William Faulkner was born William Cuthbert Falkner (1897-1962) in New Albany, Mississippi, and spent most of his life in the nearby town of Oxford. Dropping out of high school before graduating, Faulkner attended the University of Mississippi sporadically as a special student, and trained for the Royal Canadian Air Force in 1918. Although the end of World War I in November prevented him from seeing action, he later concocted elaborate stories of battle wounds. He added the "u" to his name upon publication of his first collection of poems, The Marble Faun, *in 1924. His first novel,* Soldier's Pay, *was published in 1926, followed by* Mosquitoes *in 1927 and* The Sound and the Fury *in 1929. In the decade that followed Faulkner established himself as an extraordinary and prolific writer, creating the fictional Yoknapatawpha County out of his "little postage stamp of native soil." Popular success eluded him, however, and he supported his family by writing short pieces and Hollywood screenplays. With the publication of Malcolm Cowley's* Portable Faulkner *in 1946, his reputation was revived, and he received the Nobel Prize for literature in 1950. "A Rose for Emily," one of his most popular stories, features the hauntingly grotesque characters and situations that appear in so many of his works.*

Reprinted from *Collected Short Stories of William Faulkner,* by permission of Random House, Inc. Copyright © 1958 by Williams Faulkner.

I

When Miss Emily Grierson died, our whole town went to her funeral: the men through a sort of respectful affection for a fallen monument, the women mostly out of curiosity to see the inside of her house, which no one save an old manservant—a combined gardener and cook—had seen in at least ten years.

It was a big, squarish frame house that had once been white, decorated with cupolas and spires and scrolled balconies in the heavily lightsome style of the seventies, set on what had once been our most select street. But garages and cotton gins had encroached and obliterated even the august names of that neighborhood; only Miss Emily's house was left, lifting its stubborn and coquettish decay above the cotton wagons and the gasoline pumps—an eyesore among eyesores. And now Miss Emily had gone to join the representatives of those august names where they lay in the cedar-bemused cemetery among the ranked and anonymous graves of Union and Confederate soldiers who fell at the battle of Jefferson.

Alive, Miss Emily had been a tradition, a duty, and a care; a sort of hereditary obligation upon the town, dating from that day in 1894 when Colonel Sartoris, the mayor—he who fathered the edict that no Negro woman should appear on the streets without an apron—remitted her taxes, the dispensation dating from the death of her father on into perpetuity. Not that Miss Emily would have accepted charity. Colonel Sartoris invented an involved tale to the effect that Miss Emily's father had loaned money to the town, which the town, as a matter of business, preferred this way of repaying. Only a man of Colonel Sartoris' generation and thought could have invented it, and only a woman could have believed it.

When the next generation, with its more modern ideas, became mayors and aldermen, this arrangement created some little dissatisfaction. On the first of the year they mailed her a tax notice. February came, and there was no reply. They wrote her a formal letter, asking her to call at the sheriff's office at her convenience. A week later the mayor wrote her himself, offering to call or to send his car for her, and received in reply a note on paper of an archaic shape, in a thin, flowing calligraphy in faded ink, to the effect that she no longer went out at all. The tax notice was also enclosed, without comment.

They called a special meeting of the Board of Aldermen. A deputation waited upon her, knocked at the door through which no visi-

5 tor had passed since she ceased giving china-painting lessons eight or
ten years earlier. They were admitted by the old Negro into a dim hall
from which a staircase mounted into still more shadow. It smelled of
dust and disuse—a close, dank smell. The Negro led them into the
parlor. It was furnished in heavy, leather-covered furniture. When the
Negro opened the blinds of one window, a faint dust rose sluggishly
about their thighs, spinning with slow motes in the single sun-ray. On
a tarnished gilt easel before the fireplace stood a crayon portrait of
Miss Emily's father.

They rose when she entered—a small, fat woman in black, with
a thin gold chain descending to her waist and vanishing into her belt,
leaning on an ebony cane with a tarnished gold head. Her skeleton
was small and spare; perhaps that was why what would have been
merely plumpness in another was obesity in her. She looked bloated,
like a body long submerged in motionless water, and of that pallid
hue. Her eyes, lost in the fatty ridges of her face, looked like two small
pieces of coal pressed into a lump of dough as they moved from one
face to another while the visitors stated their errand.

She did not ask them to sit. She just stood in the door and listened quietly until the spokesman came to a stumbling halt. Then
they could hear the invisible watch ticking at the end of the gold
chain.

Her voice was dry and cold. "I have no taxes in Jefferson. Colonel
Sartoris explained it to me. Perhaps one of you can gain access to the
city records and satisfy yourselves."

"But we have. We are the city authorities, Miss Emily. Didn't you
get a notice from the sheriff, signed by him?"

"I received a paper, yes," Miss Emily said. "Perhaps he considers
himself the sheriff. . . . I have no taxes in Jefferson."

10 "But there is nothing on the books to show that, you see. We must 10
go by the—"

"See Colonel Sartoris. I have no taxes in Jefferson."

"But, Miss Emily—"

"See Colonel Sartoris." (Colonel Sartoris had been dead almost
ten years.) "I have no taxes in Jefferson. Tobe!" The Negro appeared.
"Show these gentlemen out."

II

So she vanquished them, horse and foot, just as she had vanquished their fathers thirty years before about the smell. That was two years after her father's death and a short time after her sweetheart—the one we believed would marry her—had deserted her. After her father's death she went out very little; after her sweetheart went away, people hardly saw her at all. A few of the ladies had the temerity to call, but were not received, and the only sign of life about the place was the Negro man—a young man then—going in and out with a market basket.

"Just as if a man—any man—could keep a kitchen properly," the ladies said, so they were not surprised when the smell developed. It was another link between the gross, teeming world and the high and mighty Griersons.

A neighbor, a woman, complained to the mayor, Judge Stevens, eighty years old.

"But what will you have me do about it, madam?" he said.

"Why, send her word to stop it," the woman said. "Isn't there a law?"

"I'm sure that won't be necessary," Judge Stevens said. "It's probably just a snake or a rat that nigger of hers killed in the yard. I'll speak to him about it."

The next day he received two more complaints, one from a man who came in diffident deprecation. "We really must do something about it, Judge. I'd be the last one in the world to bother Miss Emily, but we've got to do something." That night the Board of Aldermen met—three graybeards and one younger man, a member of the rising generation.

"It's simple enough," he said. "Send her word to have her place cleaned up. Give her a certain time to do it in, and if she don't . . ."

"Dammit, sir," Judge Stevens said, "will you accuse a lady to her face of smelling bad?"

So the next night, after midnight, four men crossed Miss Emily's lawn and slunk about the house like burglars, sniffing along the base of the brickwork and at the cellar openings while one of them performed a regular sowing motion with his hand out of a sack slung from his shoulder. They broke open the cellar door and sprinkled lime there, and in all the outbuildings. As they recrossed the lawn, a window that had been dark was lighted and Miss Emily sat in it, the light behind her, and her upright torso motionless as that of an idol. They crept quietly across the lawn and into the shadow of the locusts that lined the street. After a week or two the smell went away.

25   That was when people had begun to feel sorry for her. People in 25 our town remembering how old lady Wyatt, her great-aunt, had gone completely crazy at last, believed that the Griersons held themselves a little too high for what they really were. None of the young men were quite good enough for Miss Emily and such. We had long thought of them as a tableau: Miss Emily a slender figure in white in the background, her father a spraddled silhouette in the foreground, his back to her and clutching a horsewhip, the two of them framed by the backflung front door. So when she got to be thirty and was still single, we were not pleased exactly, but vindicated; even with insanity in the family she wouldn't have turned down all of her chances if they had really materialized.

When her father died, it got about that the house was all that was left to her; and in a way, people were glad. At last they could pity Miss Emily. Being left alone, and a pauper, she had become humanized. Now she too would know the old thrill and the old despair of a penny more or less.

The day after his death all the ladies prepared to call at the house and offer condolence and aid, as is our custom. Miss Emily met them at the door, dressed as usual and with no trace of grief on her face. She told them that her father was not dead. She did that for three days, with the ministers calling on her, and the doctors trying to persuade her to let them dispose of the body. Just as they were about to resort to law and force, she broke down, and they buried her father quickly.

We did not say she was crazy then. We believed she had to do that. We remembered all the young men her father had driven away, and we knew that with nothing left, she would have to cling to that which had robbed her, as people will.

III

She was sick for a long time. When we saw her again, her hair was cut short, making her look like a girl, with a vague resemblance to those angels in colored church windows—sort of tragic and serene.

The town had just let the contracts for paving the sidewalks, and in the summer after her father's death they began to work. The construction company came with niggers and mules and machinery, and a foreman named Homer Barron, a Yankee—a big, dark, ready man, with a big voice and eyes lighter than his face. The little boys would follow in groups to hear him cuss the niggers, and the niggers singing in time to the rise and fall of pricks. Pretty soon he knew everybody in town. Whenever you heard a lot of laughing anywhere about the square, Homer Barron would be in the center of the group. Presently we began to see him and Miss Emily on Sunday afternoons driving in the yellow-wheeled buggy and the matched team of bays from the livery stable.

At first we were glad that Miss Emily would have an interest, because the ladies all said, "Of course a Grierson would not think seriously of a Northerner, a day laborer." But there were still others, older people, who said that even grief could not cause a real lady to forget *noblesse oblige*—without calling it *noblesse oblige*. They just said, "Poor Emily. Her kinsfolk should come to her." She had some kin in Alabama; but years ago her father had fallen out with them over the estate of old lady Wyatt, the crazy woman, and there was no communication between the two families. They had not even been represented at the funeral.

And as soon as the old people said, "Poor Emily," the whispering began. "Do you suppose it's really so?" they said to one another. "Of course it is. What else could . . ." This behind their hands; rustling of craned silk and satin behind jalousies closed upon the sun of Sunday afternoon as the thin, swift clop-clop-clop of the matched team passed: "Poor Emily."

She carried her head high enough—even when we believed that she was fallen. It was as if she demanded more than ever the recognition of her dignity as the last Grierson; as if it had wanted that touch of earthliness to reaffirm her imperviousness. Like when she bought the rat poison, the arsenic. That was over a year after they had begun to say "Poor Emily," and while the two female cousins were visiting her.

"I want some poison," she said to the druggist. She was over thirty then, still a slight woman, though thinner than usual, with cold, haughty black eyes in a face the flesh of which was strained across the temples and about the eyesockets as you imagine a lighthouse-keeper's face ought to look. "I want some poison," she said.

35 "Yes, Miss Emily. What kind? For rats and such? I'd recom—" 35
"I want the best you have. I don't care what kind."

The druggist named several. "They'll kill anything up to an elephant. But what you want is—"

"Arsenic," Miss Emily said. "Is that a good one?"

40 "Is . . . arsenic? Yes ma'am. But what you want—" 40
"I want arsenic."

The druggist looked down at her. She looked back at him, erect, her face like a strained flag. "Why, of course," the druggist said. "If that's what you want. But the law requires you to tell what you are going to use it for."

Miss Emily just stared at him, her head tilted back in order to look him eye for eye, until he looked away and went and got the arsenic and wrapped it up. The Negro delivery boy brought her the package; the druggist didn't come back. When she opened the package at home there was written on the box, under the skull and bones: "For rats."

IV

45 So the next day we all said, "She will kill herself"; and we said it 45 would be the best thing. When she had first begun to be seen with Homer Barron, we had said, "She will marry him." Then we said, "She will persuade him yet," because Homer himself had remarked—he liked men, and it was known that he drank with the younger men in the Elk's Club—that he was not a marrying man. Later we said, "Poor Emily," behind the jalousies as they passed on Sunday afternoon in the glittering buggy, Miss Emily with her head high and Homer Barron with his hat cocked and a cigar in his teeth, reins and whip in a yellow glove.

Then some of the ladies began to say that it was a disgrace to the town and a bad example to the young people. The men did not want to interfere, but at last the ladies forced the Baptist minister—Miss Emily's people were Episcopal—to call upon her. He would never divulge what happened during that interview, but he refused to go back again. The next Sunday they again drove about the streets and the following day the minister's wife wrote to Miss Emily's relations in Alabama.

So she had blood-kin under her roof again and we sat back to watch developments. At first nothing happened. Then we were sure that they had to be married. We learned that Miss Emily had been to the jeweler's and ordered a man's toilet set in silver, with the letters H.B. on each piece. Two days later we learned that she had bought a complete outfit of men's clothing, including a nightshirt, and we said "They are married." We were really glad. We were glad because the two female cousins were even more Grierson than Miss Emily had ever been.

So we were surprised when Homer Barron—the streets had been finished some time since—was gone. We were a little disappointed that there was not a public blowing-off, but we believed that he had gone on to prepare for Miss Emily's coming, or to give a chance to get rid of the cousins. (By that time it was a cabal, and we were all Miss Emily's allies to help circumvent the cousins.) Sure enough, after another week they departed. And, as we had expected all along, within three days Homer Barron was back in town. A neighbor saw the Negro man admit him at the kitchen door at dusk one evening.

And that was the last we saw of Homer Barron. And of Miss Emily for some time. The Negro man went in and out with the market basket, but the front door remained closed. Now and then we would see her at a window for a moment, as the men did that night when they sprinkled the lime, but for almost six months she did not appear on the streets. Then we knew that this was to be expected too; as if that quality of her father which had thwarted her woman's life so many times had been too virulent and too furious to die.

When we next saw Miss Emily, she had grown fat and her hair was turning gray. During the next few years it grew grayer and grayer until it attained an even pepper-and-salt iron-gray, when it ceased turning. Up to the day of her death at seventy-four it was still that vigorous iron-gray, like the hair of an active man.

From that time on her front door remained closed, save for a period of six or seven years, when she was about forty, during which she gave lessons in china-painting. She fitted up a studio in one of the downstairs rooms, where the daughters and granddaughters of Colonel Sartoris' contemporaries were sent to her with the same regularity and in the same spirit that they were sent on Sundays with a twenty-five cent piece for the collection plate. Meanwhile her taxes had been remitted.

50   Then the newer generation became the backbone and the spirit   50
of the town, and the painting pupils grew up and fell away and did
not send their children to her with boxes of color and tedious brushes
and pictures cut from the ladies' magazines. The front door closed
upon the last one and remained closed for good. When the town got
free postal delivery Miss Emily alone refused to let them fasten the
metal numbers above her door and attach a mailbox to it. She would
not listen to them.

Daily, monthly, yearly we watched the Negro grow grayer and
more stooped, going in and out with the market basket. Each December we sent her a tax notice, which would be returned by the post
office a week later, unclaimed. Now and then we would see her in one
of the downstairs windows—she had evidently shut up the top floor
of the house—like the carven torso of an idol in a niche, looking or
not looking at us, we could never tell which. Thus she passed from
generation to generation—dear, inescapable, impervious, tranquil,
and perverse.

And so she died. Fell ill in the house filled with dust and shadows, with only a doddering Negro man to wait on her. We did not
even know she was sick; we had long since given up trying to get any
information from the Negro. He talked to no one, probably not even
to her, for his voice had grown harsh and rusty, as if from disuse.

She died in one of the downstairs rooms, in a heavy walnut bed
with a curtain, her gray head propped on a pillow yellow and moldy
with age and lack of sunlight.

V

55   The Negro met the first of the ladies at the front door and let   55
them in, with their hushed, sibilant voices and their quick, curious
glances, and then he disappeared. He walked right through the house
and out the back and was not seen again.

The two female cousins came at once. They held the funeral on
the second day, with the town coming to look at Miss Emily beneath
a mass of bought flowers, with the crayon face of her father musing
profoundly above the bier and the ladies sibilant and macabre; and the
very old men—some in their brushed Confederate uniforms—on the
porch and the lawn, talking of Miss Emily as if she had been a con-
temporary of theirs, believing that they had danced with her and

courted her perhaps, confusing time with its mathematical progression, as the old do, to whom all the past is not a diminishing road, but, instead, a huge meadow which no winter ever quite touches, divided from them now by the narrow bottleneck of the most recent decade of years.

Already we knew that there was one room in the region above the stairs which no one had seen in forty years, and which would have to be forced. They waited until Miss Emily was decently in the ground before they opened it.

The violence of breaking down the door seemed to fill this room with pervading dust. A thin, acrid pall as of the tomb seemed to lie everywhere upon this room decked and furnished as for a bridal: upon the valance curtains of faded rose color, upon the rose-shaded lights, upon the dressing table, upon the delicate array of crystal and the man's toilet things backed with tarnished silver, silver so tarnished that the monogram was obscured. Among them lay a collar and tie, as if they had just been removed, which, lifted, left upon the surface a pale crescent in the dust. Upon a chair hung the suit, carefully folded; beneath it the two mute shoes and the discarded socks.

The man himself lay in the bed.

For a long while we just stood there, looking down at the profound and fleshless grin. The body had aparently once lain in the attitude of an embrace, but now the long sleep that outlasts love, that conquers even the grimace of love, had cuckolded him. What was left of him, rotted beneath what was left of the nightshirt, had become inextricable from the bed in which he lay; and upon him and upon the pillow beside him lay that even coating of the patient and biding dust.

60 Then we noticed that in the second pillow was the indentation of 60 a head. One of us lifted something from it, and leaning forward, that faint and invisible dust dry and acrid in the nostrils, we saw a long strand of iron-gray hair.

Mid-term Break

Seamus Heaney

Seamus Heaney (1939–) was born in Londonderry in Northern Ireland, studied in Belfast at St. Joseph's College, and moved to Dublin in 1976. He has won many honors as a poet, most significantly the Nobel Prize for Literature in 1995 "for works of lyrical beauty and ethical depth, which exalt everyday miracles and the living past." He has taught at Oxford, Berkeley, and Harvard. Noteworthy collections include Haw Lantern *(1987),* Seeing Things *(1991),* Selected Poems: 1966-1987 *(1990),* The Spirit Level *(1996),* Electric Light *(2001), and* District and Circle *(2006). Heaney has also written plays and essays. "Mid-term Break" was first published in 1980.*

1 I sat all morning in the college sick bay
 Counting bells knelling classes to a close.
 At two o'clock our neighbors drove me home.

 In the porch I met my father crying—
5 He had always taken funerals in his stride —
 And Big Jim Evans saying it was a hard blow.

 The baby cooed and laughed and rocked the pram
 When I came in, and I was embarrassed
 By old men standing up to shake my hand

10 And tell me they were "sorry for my trouble,"
 Whispers informed strangers I was the eldest,
 Away at school, as my mother held my hand

In hers and coughed out angry tearless sighs.
At ten o'clock the ambulance arrived
15   With the corpse, stanched and bandaged by the nurses.   15

Next morning 1 went up into the room. Snowdrops
And candles soothed the bedside; I saw him
For the first time in six weeks. Paler now,

Wearing a poppy bruise on his left temple,
20   He lay in the four foot box as in his cot.   20
No gaudy scars, the bumper knocked him clear.

A four foot box, a foot for every year.

When I Was One-and-Twenty

A. E. Housman

*Alfred Edward Housman was born in England in 1859
and died in 1936. He attended Oxford University but
failed his final examinations, probably because of an unhappy love affair, and took a job working at the Patent Office. Determined to return to the academic world, he
contributed articles to learned journals and by 1911 had
won a position as a professor of Latin at Cambridge University. Although he remained a Latin scholar all his life,
he is best remembered for his sentimental poetry, and especially for the poems of* A Shropshire Lad, *the volume from
which this poem is taken. In "When I Was One-and-
Twenty," Housman tells a sad truth about being in love
that is as hard to remember when one is older as it is to
learn when one is younger.*

1 When I was one-and-twenty   1
  I heard a wise man say,
"Give crowns and pounds and guineas
  But not your heart away;

5 Give pearls away and rubies   5
  But keep your fancy free."
But I was one-and-twenty,
  No use to talk to me.

When I was one-and-twenty
10   I heard him say again,
"The heart out of the bosom
    Was never given in vain;

'Tis paid with sighs a plenty
    And sold for endless rue."
15 And I am two-and-twenty,
    And oh, 'tis true, 'tis true.

Theme for English B

Langston Hughes

Langston Hughes (1902–1967) was born in Joplin, Missouri, and grew up in Kansas and Ohio. A poet from childhood, he attended Columbia University to study engineering but dropped out. In 1923, Hughes shipped out on a freighter to Africa, and later to Italy and France, Russia and Spain. He eventually returned to college at Lincoln University, from which he was graduated in 1929. In his long career as a writer, Hughes published sixteen books of poetry.

1 The instructor said,   1

    Go home and write
    a page tonight.
    And let that page come out of you—
5   Then, it will be true.   5

I wonder if it's that simple?
I am twenty-two, colored, born in Winston-Salem.
I went to school there, then Durham, then here
to this college on the hill above Harlem.
10 I am the only colored student in my class.   10

The steps from the hill lead down into Harlem,
through a park, then I cross St. Nicholas,
Eighth Avenue, Seventh, and I come to the Y,
the Harlem Branch Y, where I take the elevator
15 up to my room, sit down, and write this page: 15

It's not easy to know what is true for you or me
at twenty-two, my age. But I guess I'm what

"Theme for English B," by Langston Hughes, reprinted from *The Collected Poems of Langston Hughes,* edited by Arnold Rampersad and David Roessel, 1951, Alfred A. Knopf.

I feel and see and hear. Harlem, I hear you:
hear you, hear me—we too—you, me, talk on this page,
20   (I hear New York, too.) Me—who?   20

Well, I like to eat, sleep, drink, and be in love.
I like to work, read, learn, and understand life.
I like a pipe for a Christmas present,
or records—Bessie, bop, or Bach.
25   I guess being colored doesn't make me *not* like   25
the same things other folks like who are other races.
So will my page be colored that I write?
Being me, it will not be white.
But it will be
30   a part of you, instructor.   30
You are white—
yet a part of me, as I am a part of you.
That's American.
Sometimes perhaps you don't want to be a part of me
35   Nor do I often want to be a part of you.   35
But we are, that's true,
I guess you learn from me—
although you're older—and white—
and sometimes more free.

40   This is my page for English B.   40

Araby

James Joyce

James Augustine Aloysius Joyce (1882-1941) was born in
Dublin, a city he once called "the center of paralysis." He
attended Clongowes Wood College but his parents fell on
hard times and he had to leave the school; he later attended
Belevedere College on a scholarship. He describes these early
years in his short story collection Dubliners (1914) and in
his semi-autobiographical novel Portrait of the Artist as a
Young Man (1914-15). Ultimately Joyce took a degree in
modern languages from University College, Dublin, in
1902. He met his lifetime companion, Nora Barnacle, two
years later. They moved to Paris and then to Trieste, where
their son, Giorgio, and daughter, Lucia, were born. Their
travels took them from Zurich and then back to Paris,
where Joyce completed Ulysses and Finnegan's Wake, his
two most famous and ambitious novels. The German oc-
cupation of Paris in World War II forced Joyce and his family to leave for Zurich, where they lived until Joyce's death
in 1941. "Araby" is the third story in Dubliners.

1   Northern Richmond Street, being blind, was a quiet street except   1
at the hour when the Christian Brothers' School set the boys
free. An uninhabited house of two storeys stood at the blind
end, detached from its neighbours in a square ground. The other
houses of the street, conscious of decent lives within them, gazed at
one another with brown imperturbable faces.

The former tenant of our house, a priest, had died in the back
drawing room. Air, musty from having long been enclosed, hung in
all the rooms, and the waste room behind the kitchen was littered with
old useless papers. Among these I found a few paper-covered books,
the pages of which were curled and damp: The Abbott, by Walter
Scott, The Devout Communicant and The Memoirs of Vidocq. I liked
the last best because its leaves were yellow. The wild garden behind the

Araby (1914)

108

house contained a central apple-tree and a few straggling bushes under one of which I found the late tenant's rusty bicycle-pump. He had been a very charitable priest; in his will he had left all his money to institutions and the furniture of his house to his sister.

When the short days of winter came dusk fell before we had well eaten our dinners. When we met in the street the houses had grown sombre. The space of sky above us was the colour of ever-changing violet and towards it the lamps of the street lifted their feeble lanterns. The cold air stung us and we played till our bodies glowed. Our shouts echoed in the silent street. The career of our play brought us through the dark muddy lanes behind the houses where we ran the gauntlet of the rough tribes from the cottages, to the back doors of the dark dripping gardens where odours arose from the ashpits, to the dark odorous stables where a coachman smoothed and combed the horse or shook music from the buckled harness. When we returned to the street light from the kitchen windows had filled the areas. If my uncle was seen turning the corner we hid in the shadow until we had seen him safely housed. Or if Mangan's sister came out on the doorstep to call her brother in to his tea we watched her from our shadow peer up and down the street. We waited to see whether she would remain or go in and, if she remained, we left our shadow and walked up to Mangan's steps resignedly. She was waiting for us, her figure defined by the light from the half-opened door. Her brother always teased her before he obeyed and I stood by the railings looking at her. Her dress swung as she moved her body and the soft rope of her hair tossed from side to side.

Every morning I lay on the floor in the front parlor watching her door. The blind was pulled down within an inch of the sash so that I could not be seen. When she came out on the doorstep my heart leaped. I ran to the hall, seized my books and followed her. I kept her brown figure always in my eye and, when we came near the point at which our ways diverged, I quickened my pace and passed her. This happened morning after morning. I had never spoken to her, except for a few casual words, and yet her name was like a summons to all my foolish blood.

5   Her image accompanied me even in places the most hostile to romance. On Saturday evenings when my aunt went marketing I had to go to carry some of the parcels. We walked through the flaring street, jostled by drunken men and bargaining women, amid the curses of

labourers, the shrill litanies of shop-boys who stood on guard by the barrels of pigs' cheeks, the nasal chanting of street singers, who sang a come-all-you about O'Donovan Rossa, or a ballad about the troubles in our native land. These noises converged in a single sensation of life for me: I imagined that I bore my chalice safely through the throng of foes. Her name sprang to my lips at moments in strange prayers and praises which I myself did not understand. My eyes were often full of tears (I could not tell why) and at times a flood from my heart seemed to pour itself out into my bosom. I thought little of the future. I did not know whether I would ever speak to her or not or, if I spoke to her, how I could tell her of my confused adoration. But my body was like a harp and her words and gestures were like fingers running upon the wires.

One evening I went into the back drawing-room in which the priest had died. It was a dark rainy evening and there was no sound in the house. Through one of the broken panes I heard the rain impinge upon the earth, the fine incessant needles of water playing in the sodden beds. Some distant lamp or lighted window gleamed below me. I was thankful that I could see so little. All my senses seemed to desire to veil themselves and, feeling that I was about to slip from them, I pressed the palms of my hands together until they trembled, murmuring: "0 love! 0 love!" many times.

At last she spoke to me. When she addressed the first words to me I was so confused that I did not know what to answer. She asked me was I going to Araby. I forget whether I answered yes or no. It would be a splendid bazaar, she said; she would love to go.

—And why can't you? I asked.

While she spoke she turned a silver bracelet round and round her wrist. She could not go, she said, because there would be a retreat that week in her convent. Her brother and two other boys were fighting for their caps and I was alone at the railings. She held one of the spikes, bowing her head towards me. The light from the lamp opposite our door caught the white curve of her neck, lit up her hair that rested there and, falling, lit up the hand upon the railing. It fell over one side of her dress and caught the white border of a petticoat, just visible as she stood at ease.

10 —It's well for you, she said.   10

—If I go, I said, I will bring you something.

What innumerable follies laid waste my waking and sleeping thoughts after that evening! I wished to annihilate the tedious intervening days. I chafed against the work of school. At night in my bedroom and by day in the classroom her image came between me and the page I strove to read. The syllables of the word Araby were called to me through the silence in which my soul luxuriated and cast an Eastern enchantment over me. I asked for leave to go to the bazaar on Saturday night. My aunt was surprised and hoped it was not some Freemason affair. I answered few questions in class. I watched my master's face pass from amiability to sternness; he hoped I was not beginning to idle. I could not call my wandering thoughts together. I had hardly any patience with the serious work of life which, now that it stood between me and my desire, seemed to me child's play, ugly monotonous child's play.

On Saturday morning I reminded my uncle that I wished to go to the bazaar in the evening. He was fussing at the hallstand, looking for the hatbrush, and answered me curtly:

—Yes, boy, I know.

As he was in the hall I could not go into the front parlour and lie at the window. I left the house in bad humour and walked slowly towards the school. The air was pitilessly raw and already my heart misgave me.

When I came home to dinner my uncle had not yet been home. Still, it was early. I sat staring at the clock for some time and, when its ticking began to irritate me, I left the room. I mounted the staircase and gained the upper part of the house. The high cold empty gloomy rooms liberated me and I went from room to room singing. From the front window I saw my companions playing below in the street. Their cries reached me weakened and indistinct and, leaning my forehead against the cool glass, I looked over at the dark house where she lived. I may have stood there for an hour, seeing nothing but the brown-clad figure cast by my imagination, touched discreetly by the lamplight at the curved neck, at the hand upon the railing and at the border below the dress.

When I came downstairs again I found Mrs. Mercer sitting at the fire. She was an old garrulous woman, a pawnbroker's widow, who collected used stamps for some pious purpose. I had to endure the gossip of the tea-table. The meal was prolonged beyond an hour and still my uncle did not come. Mrs. Mercer stood up to go: she was sorry she couldn't wait any longer, but it was after eight o'clock and she did not like to be out late, as the night air was bad for her. When she had gone I began to walk up and down the room, clenching my fists. My aunt said:

—I'm afraid you may put off your bazaar for this night of Our Lord.

At nine o'clock I heard my uncle's latchkey in the halldoor. I heard him talking to himself and heard the hallstand rocking when it had received the weight of his overcoat. I could interpret these signs. When he was midway through his dinner I asked him to give me the money to go to the bazaar. He had forgotten.

20 —The people are in bed and after their first sleep now, he said. 20

I did not smile. My aunt said to him energetically:

—Can't you give him the money and let him go? You've kept him late enough as it is.

My uncle said he was very sorry he had forgotten. He said he believed in the old saying: "All work and no play makes Jack a dull boy." He asked me where I was going and, when I had told him a second time he asked me did I know The Arab's Farewell to his Steed. When I left the kitchen he was about to recite the opening lines of the piece to my aunt.

I held a florin tightly in my hand as I strode down Buckingham Street towards the station. The sight of the streets thronged with buyers and glaring with gas recalled to me the purpose of my journey. I took my seat in a third-class carriage of a deserted train. After an intolerable delay the train moved out of the station slowly. It crept onward among ruinous houses and over the twinkling river. At Westland Row Station a crowd of people pressed to the carriage doors; but the porters moved them back, saying that it was a special train for the bazaar. I remained alone in the bare carriage. In a few minutes the train drew up beside an improvised wooden platform. I passed out on to the road and saw by the lighted dial of a clock that it was ten minutes to ten. In front of me was a large building which displayed the magical name.

25 I could not find any sixpenny entrance and, fearing that the 25 bazaar would be closed, I passed in quickly through a turnstile, handing a shilling to a weary-looking man. I found myself in a big hall girdled at half its height by a gallery. Nearly all the stalls were closed and the greater part of the hall was in darkness. I recognized a silence like

that which pervades a church after a service. I walked into the centre of the bazaar timidly. A few people were gathered about the stalls which were still open. Before a curtain, over which the words Café Chantant were written in coloured lamps, two men were counting money on a salver. I listened to the fall of the coins.

Remembering with difficulty why I had come I went over to one of the stalls and examined porcelain vases and flowered tea-sets. At the door of the stall a young lady was talking and laughing with two young gentlemen. I remarked their English accents and listened vaguely to their conversation.

—O, I never said such a thing!

—O, but you did!

—O, but I didn't!

—Didn't she say that?

—Yes I heard her.

—O, there's a. . . fib!

Observing me the young lady came over and asked me did I wish to buy anything. The tone in her voice was not encouraging; she seemed to have spoken to me out of a sense of duty. I looked humbly at the great jars that stood like eastern guards at either side of the dark entrance to the stall and murmured:

—No, thank you.

The young lady changed the position of one of the vases and went back to the two young men. They began to talk of the same subject. Once or twice the young lady glanced at me over her shoulder.

I lingered before her stall, though I knew my stay was useless, to make my interest in her wares seem the more real. Then I turned away slowly and walked down the middle of the bazaar. I allowed the two pennies to fall against the sixpence in my pocket. I heard a voice call from one end of the gallery that the light was out. The upper part of the hall was now completely dark.

Gazing up into the darkness I saw myself as a creature driven and derided by vanity; and my eyes burned with anguish and anger.

30

35

The Ones Who Walk Away from Omelas

Ursula K. Le Guin

Ursula K. Le Guin (1929–), born Ursula Kroeber in Berkeley, California, enjoyed an intellectually stimulating childhood with her parents, anthropologist Alfred Kroeber and writer Theodora Kroeber, author of Ishi. *She received her undergraduate degree from Radcliffe College and did graduate work at Columbia University. In Paris in 1953, she married Charles A. Le Guin, a historian; in 1958 they moved to Portland, Oregon. Ursula Le Guin writes poetry and prose, especially science fiction and fantasy. Her best known fantasy works are the first four books of* Earthsea. *Her science fiction novel,* The Left Hand of Darkness *(1969), investigates gender roles with great complexity.* The Dispossessed *(1974) and* Always Coming Home *(1985) provide a new view of utopian fiction. Her* Lathe of Heaven *(1971) was made into a powerful and artistically successful science fiction movie. Recent publications include* Changing Planes *(2003);* The Wave in the Mind: Talks and Essays on the Reader, the Writer, and the Imagination *(2004); and* Gifts, *a fantasy novel, published in September 2004.*

This science fiction story introduces the reader to a planned community in which all are happy and well fed. Under the city, however, lies something so hideous that young people of conscience walk away when they see the truth.

First appeared in *New Dimensions.* Reprinted by permission from the author and the Virginia Kidd Literary Agency, Inc. Copyright © 1973, 2001 by Ursula K. Le Guin.

1   With a clamor of bells that set the swallows soaring, the   1
Festival of Summer came to the city. Omelas, bright-
towered by the sea. The rigging of the boats in harbor
sparkled with flags. In the streets between houses with red roofs and
painted walls, between old moss-grown gardens and under avenues of
trees, past great parks and public buildings, processions moved. Some
were decorous: old people in long stiff robes of mauve and grey, grave
master workmen, quiet, merry women carrying their babies and chat-
ting as they walked. In other streets the music beat faster, a shimmering of gong and tambourine, and the people went dancing, the
procession was a dance. Children dodged in and out, their high calls
rising like the swallows' crossing flights over the music and the singing.
All the processions wound towards the north side of the city, where on
the great water-meadow called the Green Fields boys and girls, naked
in the bright air, with mud-stained feet and ankles and long, lithe
arms, exercised their restive horses before the race. The horses wore no
gear at all but a halter without bit. Their manes were braided with
streamers of silver, gold, and green. They flared their nostrils and
pranced and boasted to one another; they were vastly excited, the
horse being the only animal who has adopted our ceremonies as his
own. Far off to the north and west the mountains stood up half encircling Omelas on her bay. The air of morning was so clear that the
snow still crowning the Eighteen Peaks burned with white gold fire
across the miles of sunlit air, under the dark blue of the sky. There was
just enough wind to make the banners that marked the racecourse
snap and flutter now and then. In the silence of the broad green mead-
ows one could hear the music winding through the city streets, farther
and nearer and ever approaching, a cheerful faint sweetness of the air
that from time to time trembled and gathered together and broke out
into the great joyous clanging of the bells.

Joyous! How is one to tell about joy? How describe the citizens of
Omelas?

They were not simple folk, you see, though they were happy. But we
do not say the words of cheer much any more. All smiles have become
archaic. Given a description such as this one tends to make certain
assumptions. Given a description such as this one tends to look next for
the King, mounted on a splendid stallion and surrounded by his noble
knights, or perhaps in a golden litter borne by great-muscled slaves. But
there was no king. They did not use swords, or keep slaves. They were

not barbarians. I do not know the rules and laws of their society, but I suspect that they were singularly few. As they did without monarchy and slavery, so they also got on without the stock exchange, the advertisement, the secret police, and the bomb. Yet I repeat that these were not simple folk, nor dulcet shepherds, noble savages, bland utopians. They were not less complex than us. The trouble is that we have a bad habit, encouraged by pedants and sophisticates, of considering happiness as something rather stupid. Only pain is intellectual, only evil interesting. This is the treason of the artist: a refusal to admit the banality of evil and the terrible boredom of pain. If you can't lick 'em, join 'em. If it hurts, repeat it. But to praise despair is to condemn delight, to embrace violence is to lose hold of everything else. We have almost lost hold; we can no longer describe a happy man, nor make any celebration of joy. How can I tell you about the people of Omelas? They were not naïve and happy children—though their children were, in fact, happy. They were mature, intelligent, passionate adults whose lives were not wretched. O miracle! but I wish I could describe it better. I wish I could convince you. Omelas sounds in my words like a city in a fairy tale, long ago and far away, once upon a time. Perhaps it would be best if you imagined it as your own fancy bids, assuming it will rise to the occasion, for certainly I cannot suit you all. For instance, how about technology? I think that there would be no cars or helicopters in and above the streets; this follows from the fact that the people of Omelas are happy people. Happiness is based on a just discrimination of what is necessary, what is neither necessary nor destructive, and what is destructive. In the middle category, however—that of the unnecessary but indestructive, that of comfort, luxury, exuberance, etc.—they could perfectly well have central heating, subway trains, washing machines, and all kinds of marvelous devices not yet invented here, floating light-sources, fuelless power, a cure for the commonn cold. Or they could have none of that it doesn't matter. As you like it. I incline to think that people from towns up and down the coast have been coming in to Omelas during the last days before the Festival on very fast little trains and double-decked trams and that the train station of Omelas is actually the handsomest building in town, though plainer than the magnificent Farmers' Market. But even granted trains, I fear that Omelas so far strikes some of you as goody-goody. Smiles, bells, parades, horses, bleh. If so, please add an orgy. If an orgy would help, don't hesitate. Let us not, however, have temples from which issue beautiful nude priests and priestesses already half in ecstasy and ready to copulate with any man or woman, lover or stranger, who desires union with the deep godhead of the blood, although that was my first idea. But really it would be better not to have any temples in Omelas—at least, not manned temples. Religion yes, clergy no. Surely the beautiful nudes can just wander about, offering themselves like divine soufflés to the hunger of the needy and the rapture of the flesh. Let them join the processions. Let tambourines be struck above the copulations, and the glory of desire be proclaimed upon the gongs, and (a not unimportant point) let the offspring of these delightful rituals be beloved and looked after by all. One thing I know there is none of in Omelas is guilt. But what else should there be? I thought at first there were no drugs, but that is puritanical. For those who like it, the faint insistent sweetness of *drooz* may perfume the ways of the city, drooz which first brings a great lightness and brilliance to the mind and limbs, and then after some hours a dreamy languor, and wonderful visions at last of the very arcana and inmost secrets of the Universe, as well as exciting the pleasure of sex beyond all belief; and it is not habit-forming. For more modest tastes I think there ought to be beer. What else, what else belongs in the joyous city? The sense of victory, surely, the celebration of courage. But as we did without clergy, let us do without soldiers. The joy built upon successful slaughter is not the right kind of joy; it will not do; it is fearful and it is trivial. A boundless and generous contentment, a magnanimous triumph felt not against some outer enemy but in communion with the finest and fairest in the souls of all men everywhere and the splendor of the world's summer: this is what swells the hearts of the people of Omelas, and the victory they celebrate is that of life. I really don't think many of them need to take *drooz*.

Most of the processions have reached the Green Fields by now. A marvelous smell of cooking goes forth from the red and blue tents of the provisioners. The faces of small children are amiably sticky; in the benign grey beard of a man a couple of crumbs of rich pastry are entangled. The youths and girls have mounted their horses and are beginning to group around the starting line of the course. An old woman, small, fat, and laughing, is passing out flowers from a basket, and tall young men wear her flowers in their shining hair. A child of nine or ten sits at the edge of the crowd, alone, playing on a wooden flute. People pause to listen, and they smile, but they do not speak to him, for he never ceases playing and never sees them, his dark eyes wholly rapt in the sweet, thin magic of the tune.

5   He finishes, and slowly lowers his hands holding the wooden   5
flute.

As if that little private silence were the signal, all at once a trumpet
sounds from the pavillion near the starting line: imperious, melancholy,
piercing. The horses rear on their slender legs, and some of them neigh
in answer. Sober-faced, the young riders stroke the horses' necks and
soothe them, whispering, "Quiet, quiet, there my beauty, my hope. . . ."
They begin to form in rank along the starting line. The crowds along the
racecourse are like a field of grass and flowers in the wind. The Festival of
Summer has begun.

Do you believe? Do you accept the festival, the city, the joy? No?
Then let me describe one more thing.

In a basement under one of the beautiful public buildings of
Omelas, or perhaps in the cellar of one of its spacious private homes,
there is a room. It has one locked door, and no window. A little light
seeps in dustily between cracks in the boards, secondhand from a cob-
webbed window somewhere across the cellar. In one corner of the little
room a couple of mops, with stiff, clotted, foul-smelling heads, stand
near a rusty bucket. The floor is dirt, a little damp to the touch, as cellar dirt usually is. The room is about three paces long and two wide: a
mere broom closet or disused tool room. In the room a child is sitting.
It could be a boy or a girl. It looks about six, but actually is nearly ten.
It is feeble-minded. Perhaps it was born defective, or perhaps it has
become imbecile through fear, malnutrition, and neglect. It picks its
nose and occasionally fumbles vaguelly with its toes or genitals, as it
sits hunched in the corner farthest from the bucket and the two mops.
It is afraid of the mops. It finds them horrible. It shuts its eyes, but it
knows the mops are still standing there; and the door is locked; and
nobody will come. The door is always locked; and nobody ever comes,
except that sometimes—the child has no understanding of time or
interval—sometimes the door rattles terribly and opens, and a person,
or several people, are there. One of them may come in and kick the
child to make it stand up. The others never come close, but peer in at
it with frightened, disgusted eyes. The food bowl and the water jug are
hastily filled, the door is locked, the eyes disappear. The people at the
door never say anything, but the child, who has not always lived in the
tool room, and can remember sunlight and its mother's voice, sometimes speaks. "I will be good," it says. "Please let me out. I will be
good!" They never answer. The child used to scream for help at night,

and cry a good deal, but now it only makes a kind of whining, "eh-haa, eh-haa," and it speaks less and less often. It is so thin there are no calves to its legs; its belly protrudes; it lives on a half-bowl of corn meal and grease a day. It is naked. Its buttocks and thighs are a mass of festered sores, as it sits in its own excrement continually.

They all know it is there, all the people of Omelas. Some of them have come to see it, others are content merely to know it is there. They all know that it has to be there. Some of them understand why, and some do not, but they all understand that their happiness, the beauty of their city, the tenderness of their friendships, the health of their children, the wisdom of their scholars, the skill of their makers, even the abundance of their harvest and the kindly weathers of their skies, depend wholly on this child's abominable misery.

10   This is usually explained to children when they are between eight   10 and twelve, whenever they seem capable of understanding; and most of those who come to see the child are young people, though often enough an adult comes, or comes back, to see the child. No matter how well the matter has been explained to them, these young spectators are always shocked and sickened at the sight. They feel disgust, which they had thought themselves superior to. They feel anger, outrage, impotence, despite all the explanations. They would like to do something for the child. But there is nothing they can do. If the child were brought up into the sunlight out of that vile place, if it were cleaned and fed and comforted, that would be a good thing, indeed; but if it were done, in that day and hour all the prosperity and beauty and delight of Omelas would wither and be destroyed. Those are the terms. To exchange all the goodness and grace of every life in Omelas for that single, small improvement: to throw away the happiness of thousands for the chance of the happiness of one: that would be to let guilt within the walls indeed.

The terms are strict and absolute; there may not even be a kind word spoken to the child.

Often the young people go home in tears, or in a tearless rage, when they have seen the child and faced this terrible paradox. They may brood over it for weeks or years. But as time goes on they begin to realize that even if the child could be released, it would not get much good of its freedom: a little vague pleasure of warmth and food, no doubt, but little more. It is too degraded and imbecile to know any real joy. It has been afraid too long ever to be free of fear. Its habits are too uncouth for it to respond to humane treatment. Indeed, after so long it would probably be wretched without walls about it to protect it, and darkness for its eyes, and its own excrement to sit in. Their tears at the bitter injustice dry when they begin to perceive the terrible justice of reality and to accept it. Yet it is their tears and anger, the trying of their generosity and the acceptance of their helplessness, which are perhaps the true source of the splendor of their lives. Theirs is no vapid, irresponsible happiness. They know that they, like the child, are not free. They know compassion. It is the existence of the child, and their knowledge of its existence, that makes possible the nobility of their archi-tecture, the poignancy of their music, the profundity of their science. It is because of the child that they are so gentle with children. They know that if the wretched one were not there snivelling in the dark, the other one, the flute-player, could make no joyful music as the young riders line up in their beauty for the race in the sunlight of the first morning of summer.

Now do you believe in them? Are they not more credible? But there is one more thing to tell, and this is quite incredible.

At times one of the adolescent girls or boys who go to see the child does not go home to weep or rage, does not, in fact, go home at all. Sometimes also a man or woman much older falls silent for a day or two, and then leaves home. These people go out into the street, and walk down the street alone. They keep walking, and walk straight out of the city of Omelas, through the beautiful gates. They keep walking across the farmlands of Omelas. Each one goes alone, youth or girl, man or woman. Night falls; the traveler must pass down village streets, between the houses with yellow-lit windows, and on out into the darkness of the fields. Each alone, they go west or north, towards the mountains. They go on. They leave Omelas, they walk ahead into the darkness, and they do not come back. The place they go towards is a place even less imagin-able to most of us than the city of happiness. I cannot describe it at all. It is possible that it does not exist. But they seem to know where they are going, the ones who walk away from Omelas.

Texts
Ursula K. Le Guin

Born in 1929 in Berkeley, California, Ursula K. Le Guin is one of America's most prolific and versatile writers, although particularly noted for her works of fantasy and science fiction. She was raised in an academic family. Her father was a well-known anthropologist and her mother was the author of an influential book on the Yana Indians. Le Guin's list of awards is commanding. She has won the National Book Award and a Newberry Honor. Also, she has won the Hugo and Nebula Awards numerous times, solidifying her place as perhaps the most acknowledged writer of fantasy and science fiction. A few of her most recent works are Sixty Odd: New Poems *(1999),* Tao Te Ching: A Book About the Way and the Power of the Way *(1997),* The Twins, the Dream: Two Voices *(1996), and* Unlocking the Air and Other Stories *(1996). The following selection is from* Searoad: Chronicles of Klatsand *(1990). It tells the story of a woman who attempts to understand the language of the sea.*

1 Messages came, Johanna thought, usually years too late, or years before one could crack their code or had even learned the language they were in. Yet they came increasingly often and were so urgent, so compelling in their demand that she read them, that she do something, as to force her at last to take refuge from them. She rented, for the month of January, a little house with no telephone in a seaside town that had no mail delivery. She had stayed there several times in summer; winter, as she had hoped, was even quieter than summer. A whole day would go by without her hearing or speaking a

word. She did not buy the paper or turn on the television, and the one morning she thought she ought to find some news on the radio she got a program in Finnish from Astoria. But the messages still came. Words were everywhere.

Literate clothing was no real problem. She remembered the first print dress she had ever seen, years ago, a genuine *print* dress with typography involved in the design—green on white, suitcases and hibiscus and the names *Riviera* and *Capri* and *Paris* occurring rather blobbily from shoulder-seam to hem, sometimes right side up, sometimes upside down. Then it had been, as the saleswoman said, very unusual. Now it was hard to find a T-shirt that did not urge political action, or quote lengthily from a dead physicist, or at least mention the town it was for sale in. All this she had coped with, she had even worn. But too many things were becoming legible.

She had noticed in earlier years that the lines of foam left by waves on the sand after stormy weather lay sometimes in curves that looked like handwriting, cursive lines broken by spaces, as if in words; but it was not until she had been alone for over a fortnight and had walked many times down to Wreck Point and back that she found she could read the writing. It was a mild day, nearly windless, so that she did not have to march briskly but could mosey along between the foam-lines and water's edge where the sand reflected the sky. Every now and then a quiet winter breaker driving up and up the beach would drive her and a few gulls ahead of it onto the drier sand; then as the wave receded she and the gulls would follow it back. There was not another soul on the long beach. The sand lay as firm and even as a pad of pale brown paper, and on it a recent wave at its high mark had left a complicated series of curves and bits of foam. The ribbons and loops and lengths of white looked so much like handwriting in chalk that she stopped, the way she would stop, half willingly, to read what people scratched in the sand in summer. Usually it was "Jason+Karen" or paired initials in a heart; once, mysteriously and memorably, three initials and the dates 1973–1984, the only such inscription that spoke of a promise not made but broken. Whatever those eleven years had been, the length of a marriage? a child's life? they were gone, and the letters and numbers also were gone when she came back by where they had been, with the tide rising. She had wondered then if the person who wrote them had written them to be erased. But these foam words lying on the brown sand now had been written by the erasing sea itself. If she could read them they might tell her a wisdom a good deal deeper and bitterer than she could possibly swallow. Do I want to know what the sea writes? she thought, but at the same time she was already reading the foam, which though in vaguely cuneiform blobs rather than letters of any alphabet was perfectly legible as she walked along beside it. "Yes," it read, "esse hes hetu tokye to' ossusess ekyes. Seham hute' u." (When she wrote it down later she used the apostrophe to represent a kind of stop or click like the last sound in "Yep!") As she read it over, backing up some yards to do so, it continued to say the same thing, so she walked up and down it several times and memorised it. Presently, as bubbles burst and the blobs began to shrink, it changed here and there to read, "Yes, e hes etu kye to' ossusess kye. ham te u." She felt that this was not significant change but mere loss, and kept the original text in mind. The water of the foam sank into the sand and the bubbles dried away till the marks and lines lessened into a faint lacework of dots and scraps, half legible. It looked enough like delicate bits of fancywork that she wondered if one could also read lace or crochet.

When she got home she wrote down the foam words so that she would not have to keep repeating them to remember them, and then she looked at the machine-made Quaker lace tablecloth on the little round dining table. It was not hard to read but was, as one might expect, rather dull. She made out the first line inside the border as "pith wot pith wot pith wot" interminably, with a "dub" every thirty stitches where the border pattern interrupted.

But the lace collar she had picked up at a second-hand clothes store in Portland was a different matter entirely. It was handmade, hand written. The script was small and very even. Like the Spencerian hand she had been taught fifty years ago in the first grade, it was ornate but surprisingly easy to read. "My soul must go," was the border, repeated many times, "My soul must go, my soul must go," and the fragile webs leading inward read, "sister, sister, sister, light the light." And she did not know what she was to do, or how she was to do it.

Balthazar's Marvelous Afternoon

Gabriel García Márquez

Gabriel García Márquez was born in 1928 in Aracataca, Colombia. He was the eldest child of a poor family and was reared by his maternal grandparents. He began writing in childhood and, after a period studying law, took up writing as a profession with very little success. His breakthrough novel One Hundred Years of Solitude *(1967), written in a creative burst that lasted eighteen months, drove him deeply into debt, and nearly ruined his health. He won the Nobel Prize for Literature in 1982. In this story, he describes the life of an artist and the drives that motivate and sometimes obsess the imaginative person who must be creative.*

1   The cage was finished. Balthazar hung it under the eave, from force of habit, and when he finished lunch everyone was already saying that it was the most beautiful cage in the world. So many people came to see it that a crowd formed in front of the house, and Balthazar had to take it down and close the shop.

"You have to shave," Ursula, his wife, told him. "You look like a Capuchin."

"It's bad to shave after lunch," said Balthazar.

He had two weeks' growth, short, hard, and bristly hair like the mane of a mule, and the general expression of a frightened boy. But it was a false expression. In February he was thirty; he had been living with Ursula for four years, without marrying her and without having children, and life had given him many reasons to be on guard but none to be frightened. He did not even know that for some people the cage he had just made was the most beautiful one in the world. For him, accustomed to making cages since childhood, it had been hardly any more difficult than the others.

5   "Then rest for a while," said the woman. "With that beard you   5 can't show yourself anywhere."

While he was resting, he had to get out of his hammock several times to show the cage to the neighbors. Ursula had paid little attention to it until then. She was annoyed because her husband had neglected the work of his carpenter's shop to devote himself entirely to the cage, and for two weeks had slept poorly, turning over and muttering incoherencies, and he hadn't thought of shaving. But her annoyance dissolved in the face of the finished cage. When Balthazar woke up from his nap, she had ironed his pants and a shirt; she had put them on a chair near the hammock and had carried the cage to the dining table. She regarded it in silence.

"How much will you charge?" she asked.

"I don't know," Balthazar answered. "I'm going to ask for thirty pesos to see if they'll give me twenty."

"Ask for fifty," said Ursula. "You've lost a lot of sleep in these two weeks. Furthermore, it's rather large. I think it's the biggest cage I've ever seen in my life."

10   Balthazar began to shave.   10

"Do you think they'll give me fifty pesos?"

"That's nothing for Mr. Chepe Montiel, and the cage is worth it," said Ursula. "You should ask for sixty."

The house lay in the stifling shadow. It was the first week of April and the heat seemed less bearable because of the chirping of the cicadas. When he finished dressing. Balthazar opened the door to the patio to cool off the house, and a group of children entered the dining room.

The news had spread. Dr. Octavio Giraldo, an old physician, happy with life but tired of his profession, thought about Balthazar's cage while he was eating lunch with his invalid wife. On the inside terrace, where they put the table on hot days, there were many flowerpots and two cages with canaries. His wife liked birds, and she liked them so much that she hated cats because they could eat them up. Thinking about her, Dr. Giraldo went to see a patient that afternoon, and when he returned he went by Balthazar's house to inspect the cage.

15   There were a lot of people in the dining room. The cage was on 15 display on the table: with its enormous dome of wire, three stories inside, with passageways and compartments especially for eating and sleeping and swings in the space set aside for the birds' recreation, it seemed like a small-scale model of a gigantic ice factory. The doctor inspected it carefully, without touching it, thinking that in effect the cage was better than its reputation, and much more beautiful than any he had ever dreamed of for his wife.

    "This is a flight of the imagination," he said. He sought out Balthazar among the group of people and, fixing his maternal eyes on him, added, "You would have been an extraordinary architect."

    Balthazar blushed.

    "Thank you," he said.

    "It's true," said the doctor. He was smoothly and delicately fat, like a woman who had been beautiful in her youth, and he had delicate hands. His voice seemed like that of a priest speaking Latin. "You wouldn't even need to put birds in it," he said, making the cage turn in front of the audience's eyes as if he were auctioning it off, "It would be enough to hang it in the trees so it could sing by itself." He put it back on the table, thought a moment, looking at the cage, and said:

20   "Fine, then I'll take it."   20

    "It's sold," said Ursula.

    "It belongs to the son of Mr. Chepe Montiel," said Balthazar. "He ordered it specially."

    The doctor adopted a respectful attitude.

    "Did he give you the design?"

25   "No," said Balthazar. "He said he wanted a large cage, like this 25 one, for a pair of troupials."

    The doctor looked at the cage.

    "But this isn't for troupials."

    "Of course it is, Doctor," said Balthazar, approaching the table. The children surrounded him. "The measurements are carefully calculated," he said, pointing to the different compartments with his forefinger. Then he struck the dome with his knuckles, and the cage filled with resonant chords.

    "It's the strongest wire you can find, and each joint is soldered outside and in," he said.

30 "It's even big enough for a parrot," interrupted one of the chil- 30
dren.

"That it is," said Balthazar.

The doctor turned his head.

"Fine, but he didn't give you the design," he said. "He gave you
no exact specifications, aside from making it a cage big enough for
troupials. Isn't that right?"

"That's right," said Balthazar.

35 "Then there's no problem," said the doctor. "One thing is a cage 35
big enough for troupials, and another is this cage. There's no proof
that this one is the one you were asked to make."

"It's this very one," said Balthazar, confused. "That's why I made
it."

The doctor made an impatient gesture.

"You could make another one," said Ursula, looking at her husband. And then, to the doctor: "You're not in any hurry."

"I promised it to my wife for this afternoon," said the doctor.

40 "I'm very sorry, Doctor," said Balthazar, "but I can't sell you some- 40
thing that's sold already."

The doctor shrugged his shoulders. Drying the sweat from his
neck with a handkerchief, he contemplated the cage silently with the
fixed, unfocused gaze of one who looks at a ship which is sailing away.

"How much did they pay you for it?"

Balthazar sought out Ursula's eyes without replying.

"Sixty pesos," she said.

45 The doctor kept looking at the cage. "It's very pretty." He sighed. 45
"Extremely pretty." Then, moving toward the door, he began to fan
himself energetically, smiling, and the trace of that episode disappeared forever from his memory.

"Montiel is very rich," he said.

In truth, José Montiel was not as rich as he seemed, but he would
have been capable of doing anything to become so. A few blocks from
there, in a house crammed with equipment, where no one had ever
smelled a smell that couldn't be sold, he remained indifferent to the
news of the cage. His wife, tortured by an obsession with death, closed
the doors and windows after lunch and lay for two hours with her eyes
opened to the shadow of the room, while José Montiel took his siesta.
The clamor of many voices surprised her there. Then she opened the
door to the living room and found a crowd in front of the house, and

Balthazar with the cage in the middle of the crowd, dressed in white, freshly shaved, with that expression of decorous candor with which the poor approach the houses of the wealthy.

"What a marvelous thing!" José Montiel's wife exclaimed, with a radiant expression, leading Balthazar inside. "I've never seen anything like it in my life," she said, and added, annoyed by the crowd which piled up at the door:

"But bring it inside before they turn the living room into a grandstand."

Balthazar was no stranger to José Montiel's house. On different occasions, because of his skill and forthright way of dealing, he had been called in to do minor carpentry jobs. But he never felt at ease among the rich. He used to think about them, about their ugly and argumentative wives, about their tremendous surgical operations, and he always experienced a feeling of pity. When he entered their houses, he couldn't move without dragging his feet.

"Is Pepe home?" he asked.

He had put the cage on the dining-room table.

"He's at school," said José Montiel's wife. "But he shouldn't be long," and she added, "Montiel is taking a bath."

In reality, José Montiel had not had time to bathe. He was giving himself an urgent alcohol rub, in order to come out and see what was going on. He was such a cautious man that he slept without an electric fan so he could watch over the noises of the house while he slept.

"Adelaide!" he shouted. "What's going on?"

"Come and see what a marvelous thing!" his wife shouted.

José Montiel, obese and hairy, his towel draped around his neck, appeared at the bedroom window.

"What is that?"

"Pepe's cage," said Balthazar.

His wife looked at him perplexedly.

"Whose?"

"Pepe's," replied Balthazar. And then, turning toward José Montiel, "Pepe ordered it."

Nothing happened at that instant, but Balthazar felt as if someone had just opened the bathroom door on him. José Montiel came out of the bedroom in his underwear.

"Pepe!" he shouted.

"He's not back," whispered his wife, motionless.

Pepe appeared in the doorway. He was about twelve, and had the same curved eyelashes and was as quietly pathetic as his mother.

"Come here," José Montiel said to him. "Did you order this?"

The child lowered his head. Grabbing him by the hair, José Montiel forced Pepe to look him in the eye.

"Answer me."

70 The child bit his lip without replying.   70

"Montiel," whispered his wife.

José Montiel let the child go and turned toward Balthazar in a fury. "I'm very sorry, Balthazar," he said. "But you should have consulted me before going on. Only to you would it occur to contract with a minor." As he spoke, his face recovered its serenity. He lifted the cage without looking at it and gave it to Balthazar.

"Take it away at once, and try to sell it to whomever you can," he said. "Above all, I beg you not to argue with me." He patted him on the back and explained, "The doctor has forbidden me to get angry."

The child had remained motionless, without blinking, until Balthazar looked at him uncertainly with the cage in his hand. Then he emitted a gutteral sound, like a dog's growl, and threw himself on the floor screaming.

75 José Montiel looked at him, unmoved, while the mother tried to   75 pacify him. "Don't even pick him up," he said. "Let him break his head on the floor, and then put salt and lemon on it so he can rage to his heart's content." The child was shrieking tearlessly while his mother held him by the wrists.

"Leave him alone," José Montiel insisted.

Balthazar observed the child as he would have observed the death throes of a rabid animal. It was almost four o'clock. At that hour, at his house, Ursula was singing a very old song and cutting slices of onion.

"Pepe," said Balthazar.

He approached the child, smiling, and held the cage out to him. The child jumped up, embraced the cage which was almost as big as he was, and stood looking at Balthazar through the wirework without knowing what to say. He hadn't shed one tear.

80 "Balthazar," said José Montiel softly. "I told you already to take it 80 away."

"Give it back," the woman ordered the child.

"Keep it," said Balthazar. And then, to José Montiel: "After all, that's what I made it for."

José Montiel followed him into the living room.

"Don't be foolish, Balthazar," he was saying, blocking his path. "Take your piece of furniture home and don't be silly. I have no intention of paying you a cent."

85 "It doesn't matter," said Balthazar. "I made it expressly as a gift for 85 Pepe. I didn't expect to charge anything for it."

As Balthazar made his way through the spectators who were blocking the door, José Montiel was shouting in the middle of the living room. He was very pale and his eyes were beginning to get red.

"Idiot!" he was shouting. "Take your trinket out of here. The last thing we need is for some nobody to give orders in my house. Son of a bitch!"

In the pool hall, Balthazar was received with an ovation. Until that moment, he thought that he had made a better cage than ever before, that he'd had to give it to the son of José Montiel so he wouldn't keep crying, and that none of these things was particularly important. But then he realized that all of this had a certain importance for many people, and he felt a little excited.

"So they give you fifty pesos for the cage."

90 "Sixty," said Balthazar. 90

"Score one for you," someone said. "You're the only one who has managed to get such a pile of money out of Mr. Chepe Montiel. We have to celebrate."

They bought him a beer, and Balthazar responded with a round for everybody. Since it was the first time he had ever been out drinking, by dusk he was completely drunk, and he was talking about a fabulous project of a thousand cages, at sixty pesos each, and then of a million cages, till he had sixty million pesos. "We have to make a lot of things to sell to the rich before they die," he was saying, blind drunk. "All of them are sick, and they're going to die. They're so screwed up they can't even get angry any more." For two hours he was paying for the jukebox, which played without interruption. Everybody toasted Balthazar's health, good luck, and fortune, and the death of the rich, but at mealtime they left him alone in the pool hall.

Ursula had waited for him until eight, with a dish of fried meat covered with slices of onion. Someone told her that her husband was in the pool hall, delirious with happiness, buying beer for everyone, but she didn't believe it, because Balthazar had never got drunk. When she went to bed, almost at midnight, Balthazar was in a lighted room where there were little tables, each with four chairs, and an outdoor dance floor, where the plovers were walking around. His face was smeared with rouge, and since he couldn't take one more step, he thought he wanted to lie down with two women in the same bed. He had spent so much that he had had to leave his watch in pawn, with the promise to pay the next day. A moment later, spread-eagled in the street, he realized that his shoes were being taken off, but he didn't want to abandon the happiest dream of his life. The women who passed on their way to five-o'clock mass didn't dare look at him, thinking he was dead.

How to Tell a True War Story

Tim O'Brien

*Born in 1946 into a typical middle-class family in Min-
nesota, Tim O'Brien was the son of an elementary school
teacher and an insurance salesman who fought in the
Pacific in World War II. A political science major at
Macalester College in the 1960s, he participated in anti-
war protests and toyed with the idea of fleeing to Canada
after being drafted in 1969. Instead, he became an
infantry soldier in Vietnam, earning a Purple Heart for a
shrapnel wound. Upon his return, O'Brien tried graduate
school and journalism, eventually devoting himself to
writing. The central focus of all of O'Brien's work is his
Vietnam experience. His first work, the memoir If I Die
in a Combat Zone, Box Me Up and Send Me Home, was
published in 1973, and his novel Going After Cacciato
won the National Book Award in 1978. A later collection
of interrelated short stories, The Things They Carried, was
a finalist for the National Book Critics Circle Award and
the Pulitzer Prize in 1990. The narrator in this story, a
vietnam veteran, recounts a number of horrors that may
or may not have happened, attempting to explain what a
true war story is.*

1   This is true.
     I had a buddy in Vietnam. His name was Bob Kiley, but
everybody called him Rat.
     A friend of his gets killed, so about a week later Rat sits down and
writes a letter to the guy's sister. Rat tells her what a great brother she
had, how together the guy was, a number one pal and comrade. A real

Reprinted from *The Things They Carried* (1990), by permission of Houghton Mifflin
Harcourt Company.

soldier's soldier, Rat says. Then he tells a few stories to make the point, how her brother would always volunteer for stuff nobody else would volunteer for in a million years, dangerous stuff, like doing recon or going out on these really badass night patrols. Stainless steel balls, Rat tells her. The guy was a little crazy, for sure, but crazy in a good way, a real daredevil, because he liked the challenge of it, he liked testing himself, just man against gook. A great, great guy, Rat says.

Anyway, it's a terrific letter, very personal and touching. Rat almost bawls writing it. He gets all teary telling about the good times they had together, how her brother made the war seem almost fun, always raising hell and lighting up villes and bringing smoke to bear every which way. A great sense of humor, too. Like the time at this river when he went fishing with a whole damn crate of hand grenades. Probably the funniest thing in world history, Rat says, all that gore, about twenty zillion dead gook fish. Her brother, he had the right attitude. He knew how to have a good time. On Halloween, this real hot spooky night, the dude paints up his body all different colors and puts on this weird mask and hikes over to a ville and goes trick-or-treating almost stark naked, just boots and balls and an M-16. A tremendous human being, Rat says. Pretty nutso sometimes, but you could trust him with your life.

And then the letter gets very sad and serious. Rat pours his heart out. He says he loved the guy. He says the guy was his best friend in the world. They were like soul mates, he says, like twins or something, they had a whole lot in common. He tells the guy's sister he'll look her up when the war's over.

So what happens?

Rat mails the letter. He waits two months. The dumb cooze never writes back.

A true war story is never moral. It does not instruct, nor encourage virtue, nor suggest models of proper human behavior, nor restrain men from doing the things men have always done. If a story seems moral, do not believe it. If at the end of a war story you feel uplifted, or if you feel that some small bit of rectitude has been salvaged from the larger waste, then you have been made the victim of a very old and terrible lie. There is no rectitude whatsoever. There is no virtue.

As a first rule of thumb, therefore, you can tell a true war story by its absolute and uncompromising allegiance to obscenity and evil. Listen to Rat Kiley. Cooze, he says. He does not say bitch. He certainly does not say woman, or girl. He says cooze. Then he spits and stares. He's nineteen years old—it's too much for him—so he looks at you with those big sad gentle killer eyes and says *cooze,* because his friend is dead, and because it's so incredibly sad and true: she never wrote back.

You can tell a true war story if it embarrasses you. If you don't care for obscenity, you don't care for the truth; if you don't care for the truth, watch how you vote. Send guys to war, they come home talking dirty.

10 Listen to Rat: "Jesus Christ, man, I write this beautiful fuckin' 10 letter, I slave over it, and what happens? The dumb cooze never writes back."

The dead guy's name was Curt Lemon. What happened was, we crossed a muddy river and marched west into the mountains, and on the third day we took a break along a trail junction in deep jungle. Right away, Lemon and Rat Kiley started goofing. They didn't understand about the spookiness. They were kids; they just didn't know. A nature hike, they thought, not even a war, so they went off into the shade of some giant trees—quadruple canopy, no sunlight at all—and they were giggling and calling each other yellow mother and playing a silly game they'd invented. The game involved smoke grenades, which were harmless unless you did stupid things, and what they did was pull out the pin and stand a few feet apart and play catch under the shade of those huge trees. Whoever chickened out was a yellow mother. And if nobody chickened out, the grenade would make a light popping sound and they'd be covered with smoke and they'd laugh and dance around and then do it again.

It's all exactly true.

It happened, to *me,* nearly twenty years ago, and I still remember that trail junction and those giant trees and a soft dripping sound somewhere beyond the trees. I remember the smell of moss. Up in the canopy there were tiny white blossoms, but no sunlight at all, and I remember the shadows spreading out under the trees where Curt Lemon and Rat Kiley were playing catch with smoke grenades.

Mitchell Sanders sat flipping his yo-yo. Norman Bowker and Kiowa and Dave Jensen were dozing, or half dozing, and all around us were those ragged green mountains.

Except for the laughter things were quiet.

15   At one point, I remember, Mitchell Sanders turned and looked at   15 me, not quite nodding, as if to warn me about something, as if he already *knew*, then after a while he rolled up his yo-yo and moved away.

It's hard to tell you what happened next.

They were just goofing. There was a noise, I suppose, which must've been the detonator, so I glanced behind me and watched Lemon step from the shade into bright sunlight. His face was suddenly brown and shining. A handsome kid, really. Sharp gray eyes, lean and narrow-waisted, and when he died it was almost beautiful, the way the sunlight came around him and lifted him up and sucked him high into a tree full of moss and vines and white blossoms.

In any war story, but especially a true one, it's difficult to separate what happened from what seemed to happen. What seems to happen becomes its own happening and has to be told that way. The angles of vision are skewed. When a booby trap explodes, you close your eyes and duck and float outside yourself. When a guy dies, like Curt Lemon, you look away and then look back for a moment and then look away again. The pictures get jumbled; you tend to miss a lot. And then afterward, when you go to tell about it, there is always that surreal seemingness, which makes the story seem untrue, but which in fact represents the hard and exact truth as it *seemed*.

*   *   *

In many cases a true war story cannot be believed. If you believe it, be skeptical. It's a question of credibility. Often the crazy stuff is true and the normal stuff isn't, because the normal stuff is necessary to make you believe the truly incredible craziness.

20   In other cases you can't even tell a true war story. Sometimes it's   20 just beyond telling.

I heard this one, for example, from Mitchell Sanders. It was near dusk and we were sitting at my foxhole along a wide muddy river north of Quang Ngai. I remember how peaceful the twilight was. A deep pinkish red spilled out on the river, which moved without sound, and in the morning we would cross the river and march west into the mountains. The occasion was right for a good story.

"God's truth," Mitchell Sanders said. "A six-man patrol goes up into the mountains on a basic listening-post operation. The idea's to spend a week up there, just lie low and listen for enemy movement. They've got a radio along, so if they hear anything suspicious—anything—they're supposed to call in artillery or gunships, whatever it takes. Otherwise they keep strict field discipline. Absolute silence. They just listen."

Sanders glanced at me to make sure I had the scenario. He was playing with his yo-yo, dancing it with short, tight little strokes of the wrist.

His face was blank in the dusk.

25 "We're talking regulation, by-the-book LP. These six guys, they 25 don't say boo for a solid week. They don't got tongues. *All* ears."

"Right," I said.

"Understand me?"

"Invisible."

Sanders nodded.

30 "Affirm," he said. "Invisible. So what happens is, these guys get 30 themselves deep in the bush, all camouflaged up, and they lie down and wait and that's all they do, nothing else, they lie there for seven straight days and just listen. And man, I'll tell you—it's spooky. This is mountains. You don't *know* spooky till you been there. Jungle, sort of, except it's way up in the clouds and there's always this fog—like rain, except it's not raining—everything's all wet and swirly and tangled up and you can't see jack, you can't find your own pecker to piss with. Like you don't even have a body. Serious spooky. You just go with the vapors—the fog sort of takes you in . . . And the sounds, man. The sounds carry forever. You hear stuff nobody should *ever* hear."

Sanders was quiet for a second, just working the yo-yo, then he smiled at me.

"So after a couple days the guys start hearing this real soft, kind of wacked-out music. Weird echoes and stuff. Like a radio or something, but it's not a radio, it's this strange gook music that comes right out of the rocks. Faraway, sort of, but right up close, too. They try to ignore it. But it's a listening post, right? So they listen. And every night they keep hearing that crazyass gook concert. All kinds of chimes and xylophones. I mean, this is wilderness—no way, it can't be real—but there it *is*, like the mountains are tuned in to Radio fucking Hanoi. Naturally they get nervous. One guy sticks Juicy Fruit in his ears. Another guy almost flips. Thing is, though, they can't report music. They can't get on the horn and call back to base and say, 'Hey, listen, we need some firepower, we got to blow away this weirdo gook rock band.' They can't do that. It wouldn't go down. So they lie there in the fog and keep their mouths shut. And what makes it extra bad, see, is the poor dudes can't horse around like normal. Can't joke it away. Can't even talk to each other except maybe in whispers, all hush-hush, and that just revs up the willies. All they do is listen."

Again there was some silence as Mitchell Sanders looked out on the river. The dark was coming on hard now, and off to the west I could see the mountains rising in silhouette, all the mysteries and unknowns.

"This next part," Sanders said quietly, "you won't believe."

"Probably not," I said.

"You won't. And you know why?" He gave me a long, tired smile. "Because it happened. Because every word is absolutely dead-on true."

Sanders made a sound in his throat, like a sigh, as if to say he didn't care if I believed him or not. But he did care. He wanted me to feel the truth, to believe by the raw force of feeling. He seemed sad, in a way.

"These six guys," he said, "they're pretty fried out by now, and one night they start hearing voices. Like at a cocktail party. That's what it sounds like, this big swank gook cocktail party somewhere out there in the fog. Music and chitchat and stuff. It's crazy, I know, but they hear the champagne corks. They hear the actual martini glasses. Real hoity-toity, all very civilized, except this isn't civilization. This is Nam.

"Anyway, the guys try to be cool. They just lie there and groove, but after a while they start hearing—you won't believe this—they hear chamber music. They hear violins and cellos. They hear this terrific mama-san soprano. Then after a while they hear gook opera and a glee club and the Haiphong Boys Choir and a barbershop quartet and all kinds of weird chanting and Buddha-Buddha stuff. And the whole time, in the background, there's still that cocktail party going

35

35

137

on. All these different voices. Not human voices, though. Because it's the mountains. Follow me? The rock—it's *talking*. And the fog, too, and the grass and the goddamn mongooses. Everything talks. The trees talk politics, the monkeys talk religion. The whole country. Vietnam. The place talks. It talks. Understand? Nam—it truly *talks*.

40   "The guys can't cope. They lose it. They get on the radio and   40 report enemy movement—a whole army, they say—and they order up the firepower. They get arty and gunships. They call in air strikes. And I'll tell you, they fuckin' crash that cocktail party. All night long, they just smoke those mountains. They make jungle juice. They blow away trees and glee clubs and whatever else there is to blow away. Scorch time. They walk napalm up and down the ridges. They bring in the Cobras and F-4s, they use Willie Peter and HE and incendiaries. It's all fire. They make those mountains burn.

"Around dawn things finally get quiet. Like you never even *heard* quiet before. One of those real thick, real misty days—just clouds and fog, they're off in this special zone—and the mountains are absolutely dead-flat silent. Like Brigadoon—pure vapor, you know? Everything's all sucked up inside the fog. Not a single sound, except they still *hear* it.

"So they pack up and start humping. They head down the mountain, back to base camp, and when they get there they don't say diddly. They don't talk. Not a word, like they're deaf and dumb. Later on this fat bird colonel comes up and asks what the hell happened out there. What'd they hear? Why all the ordnance? The man's ragged out, he gets down tight on their case. I mean, they spent six trillion dollars on firepower, and this fatass colonel wants answers, he wants to know what the fuckin' story is.

"But the guys don't say zip. They just look at him for a while, sort of funny like, sort of amazed, and the whole war is right there in that stare. It says everything you can't ever say. It says, man, you got *wax* in your ears. It says, poor bastard, you'll never know—wrong frequency—you don't *even* want to hear this. Then they salute the fucker and walk away, because certain stories you don't ever tell."

You can tell a true war story by the way it never seems to end. Not then, not ever. Not when Mitchell Sanders stood up and moved off into the dark.

45   It all happened.   45

Even now, at this instant, I remember that yo-yo. In a way, I suppose, you had to be there, you had to hear it, but I could tell how desperately Sanders wanted me to believe him, his frustration at not quite getting the details right, not quite pinning down the final and definitive truth.

And I remember sitting at my foxhole that night, watching the shadows of Quang Ngai, thinking about the coming day and how we would cross the river and march west into the mountains, all the ways I might die, all the things I did not understand.

Late in the night Mitchell Sanders touched my shoulder.

"Just came to me," he whispered. "The moral, I mean. Nobody listens. Nobody hears nothin'. Like that fatass colonel. The politicians, all the civilian types. Your girlfriend. My girlfriend. Everybody's sweet little virgin girlfriend. What they need is to go out on LP. The vapors, man. Trees and rocks—you got to *listen* to your enemy."

50 And then again, in the morning, Sanders came up to me. The platoon was preparing to move out, checking weapons, going through all the little rituals that preceded a day's march. Already the lead squad had crossed the river and was filing off toward the west.

"I got a confession to make," Sanders said. "Last night, man, I had to make up a few things."

"I know that."

"The glee club. There wasn't any glee club."

"Right."

55 "No opera."

"Forget it, I understand."

"Yeah, but listen, it's still true. Those six guys, they heard wicked sound out there. They heard sound you just plain won't believe."

Sanders pulled on his rucksack, closed his eyes for a moment, then almost smiled at me. I knew what was coming.

"All right," I said, "what's the moral?"

60 "Forget it."

"No, go ahead."

For a long while he was quiet, looking away, and the silence kept stretching out until it was almost embarrassing. Then he shrugged and gave me a stare that lasted all day.

"Hear that quiet, man?" he said. "That quiet—just listen. There's your moral."

In a true war story, if there's a moral at all, it's like the thread that makes the cloth. You can't tease it out. You can't extract the meaning without unraveling the deeper meaning. And in the end, really, there's nothing much to say about a true war story, except maybe "Oh."

65   True war stories do not generalize. They do not indulge in 65 abstraction or analysis.

For example: War is hell. As a moral declaration the old truism seems perfectly true, and yet because it abstracts, because it generalizes, I can't believe it with my stomach. Nothing turns inside.

It comes down to gut instinct. A true war story, if truly told, makes the stomach believe.

This one does it for me. I've told it before—many times, many versions—but here's what actually happened.

We crossed that river and marched west into the mountains. On the third day, Curt Lemon stepped on a booby-trapped 105 round. He was playing catch with Rat Kiley, laughing, and then he was dead. The trees were thick; it took nearly an hour to cut an LZ for the dustoff.

70   Later, higher in the mountains, we came across a baby VC water 70 buffalo. What it was doing there I don't know—no farms or paddies— but we chased it down and got a rope around it and led it along to a deserted village where we set up for the night. After supper Rat Kiley went over and stroked its nose.

He opened up a can of C rations, pork and beans, but the baby buffalo wasn't interested.

Rat shrugged.

He stepped back and shot it through the right front knee. The animal did not make a sound. It went down hard, then got up again, and Rat took careful aim and shot off an ear. He shot it in the hindquarters and in the little hump at its back. He shot it twice in the flanks. It wasn't to kill; it was to hurt. He put the rifle muzzle up against the mouth and shot the mouth away. Nobody said much. The whole platoon stood there watching, feeling all kinds of things, but there wasn't a great deal of pity for the baby water buffalo. Curt Lemon was dead. Rat Kiley had lost his best friend in the world. Later in the week he would write a long personal letter to the guy's sister, who would not write back, but for now it was a question of pain. He shot off the tail. He shot away chunks of meat below the ribs.

All around us there was the smell of smoke and filth and deep greenery, and the evening was humid and very hot. Rat went to automatic. He shot randomly, almost casually, quick little spurts in the belly and butt. Then he reloaded, squatted down, and shot it in the left front knee. Again the animal fell hard and tried to get up, but this time it couldn't quite make it. It wobbled and went down sideways. Rat shot it in the nose. He bent forward and whispered something, as if talking to a pet, then he shot it in the throat. All the while the baby buffalo was silent, or almost silent, just a light bubbling sound where the nose had been. It lay very still. Nothing moved except the eyes, which were enormous, the pupils shiny black and dumb.

Rat Kiley was crying. He tried to say something, but then cradled his rifle and went off by himself.

The rest of us stood in a ragged circle around the baby buffalo. For a time no one spoke. We had witnessed something essential, something brand-new and profound, a piece of the world so startling there was not yet a name for it.

Somebody kicked the baby buffalo.

It was still alive, though just barely, just in the eyes.

"Amazing," Dave Jensen said. "My whole life, I never seen anything like it."

"Never?"

"Not hardly. Not once."

Kiowa and Mitchell Sanders picked up the baby buffalo. They hauled it across the open square, hoisted it up, and dumped it in the village well.

Afterward, we sat waiting for Rat to get himself together.

"Amazing," Dave Jensen kept saying. "A new wrinkle. I never seen it before."

Mitchell Sanders took out his yo-yo. "Well, that's Nam," he said. "Garden of Evil. Over here, man, every sin's real fresh and original."

How do you generalize?

War is hell, but that's not the half of it, because war is also mystery and terror and adventure and courage and discovery and holiness and pity and despair and longing and love. War is nasty; war is fun. War is thrilling; war is drudgery. War makes you a man; war makes you dead.

The truths are contradictory. It can be argued, for instance, that war is grotesque. But in truth war is also beauty. For all its horror, you can't help but gape at the awful majesty of combat. You stare out at tracer rounds unwinding through the dark like brilliant red ribbons. You crouch in ambush as a cool, impassive moon rises over the night-time paddies. You admire the fluid symmetries of troops on the move, the harmonies of sound and shape and proportion, the great sheets of metal-fire streaming down from a gunship, the illumination rounds, the white phosphorus, the purply orange glow of napalm, the rocket's red glare. It's not pretty, exactly. It's astonishing. It fills the eye. It commands you. You hate it, yes, but your eyes do not. Like a killer forest fire, like cancer under a microscope, any battle or bombing raid or artillery barrage has the aesthetic purity of absolute moral indifference—a powerful, implacable beauty—and a true war story will tell the truth about this, though the truth is ugly.

To generalize about war is like generalizing about peace. Almost everything is true. Almost nothing is true. At its core, perhaps, war is just another name for death, and yet any soldier will tell you, if he tells the truth, that proximity to death brings with it a corresponding proximity to life. After a firefight, there is always the immense pleasure of aliveness. The trees are alive. The grass, the soil—everything. All around you things are purely living, and you among them, and the aliveness makes you tremble. You feel an intense, out-of-the-skin awareness of your living self—your truest self, the human being you want to be and then become by the force of wanting it. In the midst of evil you want to be a good man. You want decency. You want justice and courtesy and human concord, things you never knew you wanted. There is a kind of largeness to it, a kind of godliness. Though it's odd, you're never more alive than when you're almost dead. You recognize what's valuable. Freshly, as if for the first time, you love what's best in yourself and in the world, all that might be lost. At the hour of dusk you sit at your foxhole and look out on a wide river turning pinkish red, and at the mountains beyond, and although in the morning you must cross the river and go into the mountains and do terrible things and maybe die, even so, you find yourself studying the fine colors on the river, you feel wonder and awe at the setting of the sun, and you are filled with a hard, aching love for how the world could be and always should be, but now is not.

Mitchell Sanders was right. For the common soldier, at least, war has the feel—the spiritual texture—of a great ghostly fog, thick and permanent. There is no clarity. Everything swirls. The old rules are no longer binding, the old truths no longer true. Right spills over into wrong. Order blends into chaos, love into hate, ugliness into beauty, law into anarchy, civility into savagery. The vapors suck you in. You can't tell where you are, or why you're there, and the only certainty is overwhelming ambiguity.

90   In war you lose your sense of the definite, hence your sense of 90 truth itself, and therefore it's safe to say that in a true war story nothing is ever absolutely true.

Often in a true war story there is not even a point, or else the point doesn't hit you until twenty years later, in your sleep, and you wake up and shake your wife and start telling the story to her, except when you get to the end you've forgotten the point again. And then for a long time you lie there watching the story happen in your head. You listen to your wife's breathing. The war's over. You close your eyes. You smile and think, Christ, what's the *point?*

This one wakes me up.

In the mountains that day, I watched Lemon turn sideways. He laughed and said something to Rat Kiley. Then he took a peculiar half step, moving from shade into bright sunlight, and the booby-trapped 105 round blew him into a tree. The parts were just hanging there, so Dave Jensen and I were ordered to shinny up and peel him off. I remember the white bone of an arm. I remember pieces of skin and something wet and yellow that must've been the intestines. The gore was horrible, and stays with me. But what wakes me up twenty years later is Dave Jensen singing "Lemon Tree" as we threw down the parts.

You can tell a true war story by the questions you ask. Somebody tells a story, let's say, and afterward you ask, "Is it true?" and if the answer matters, you've got your answer.

95   For example, we've all heard this one. Four guys go down a trail. 95 A grenade sails out. One guy jumps on it and takes the blast and saves his three buddies.

Is it true?

The answer matters.

You'd feel cheated if it never happened. Without the grounding reality, it's just a trite bit of puffery, pure Hollywood, untrue in the way all such stories are untrue. Yet even if it did happen—and maybe it did, anything's possible—even then you know it can't be true, because a true war story does not depend upon that kind of truth. Absolute occurrence is irrelevant. A thing may happen and be a total lie; another thing may not happen and be truer than the truth. For example: Four guys go down a trail. A grenade sails out. One guy jumps on it and takes the blast, but it's a killer grenade and everybody dies anyway. Before they die, though, one of the dead guys says, "The fuck you do *that* for?" and the jumper says, "Story of my life, man," and the other guy starts to smile but he's dead.

That's a true story that never happened.

100 Twenty years later, I can still see the sunlight on Lemon's face. I can 100 see him turning, looking back at Rat Kiley, then he laughed and took that curious half step from shade into sunlight, his face suddenly brown and shining, and when his foot touched down, in that instant, he must've thought it was the sunlight that was killing him. It was not the sunlight. It was a rigged 105 round. But if I could ever get the story right, how the sun seemed to gather around him and pick him up and lift him high into a tree, if I could somehow recreate the fatal whiteness of that light, the quick glare, the obvious cause and effect, then you would believe the last thing Curt Lemon believed, which for him must've been the final truth.

Now and then, when I tell this story, someone will come up to me afterward and say she liked it. It's always a woman. Usually it's an older woman of kindly temperament and humane politics. She'll explain that as a rule she hates war stories; she can't understand why people want to wallow in all the blood and gore. But this one she liked. The poor baby buffalo, it made her sad. Sometimes, even, there are little tears. What I should do, she'll say, is put it all behind me. Find new stories to tell.

I won't say it but I'll think it.

I'll picture Rat Kiley's face, his grief, and I'll think, *You dumb cooze.*

Because she wasn't listening.

105   It *wasn't* a war story. It was a *love* story.   105

144

But you can't say that. All you can do is tell it one more time, patiently, adding and subtracting, making up a few things to get at the real truth. No Mitchell Sanders, you tell her. No Lemon, no Rat Kiley. No trail junction. No baby buffalo. No vines or moss or white blossoms. Beginning to end, you tell her, it's all made up. Every goddamn detail—the mountains and the river and especially that poor dumb baby buffalo. None of it happened. *None* of it. And even if it did happen, it didn't happen in the mountains, it happened in this little village on the Batangan Peninsula, and it was raining like crazy, and one night a guy named Stink Harris woke up screaming with a leech on his tongue. You can tell a true war story if you just keep on telling it.

And in the end, of course, a true war story is never about war. It's about sunlight. It's about the special way that dawn spreads out on a river when you know you must cross the river and march into the mountains and do things you are afraid to do. It's about love and memory. It's about sorrow. It's about sisters who never write back and people who never listen.

Daddy

Sylvia Plath

Sylvia Plath (1932-1963) grew up in Boston, the daughter of a Boston University entomologist who died when she was eight years old. Plath was a good student, as children of university faculty often are, but she sometimes found herself unable to go on with her writing or her academic work. She attended Smith College, where she was graduated summa cum laude. She then earned a Fulbright Scholarship to Oxford where she met the English poet, Ted Hughes, whom she quickly married. Her poetry and her one novel, The Bell Jar *(1963), indicate the stresses in her life and her marriage. Separated and living with her two small children in a flat in London, she succumbed to those stresses and committed suicide in 1963. Her books of poetry include* A Winter Ship *(1960) and* The Colossus and Other Poems *(1960). "Daddy" (1962) embodies some of the more negative features of feminist attitudes but also expresses a kind of anger that many women suppress.*

1   You do not do, you do not do
    Any more, black shoe
    In which I have lived like a foot
    For thirty years, poor and white,
5   Barely daring to breathe or Achoo.

    Daddy, I have had to kill you.
    You died before I had time——
    Marble-heavy, a bag full of God,
    Ghastly statue with one grey toe
10 Big as a Frisco seal

And a head in the freakish Atlantic
Where it pours bean green over blue
In the waters off beautiful Nauset.
I used to pray to recover you.
Ach, du.

In the German tongue, in the Polish town
Scraped flat by the roller
Of wars, wars, wars.
But the name of the town is common.
My Polack friend

Says there are a dozen or two.
So I never could tell where you
Put your foot, your root,
I never could talk to you.
The tongue stuck in my jaw.

It stuck in a barb wire snare.
Ich, ich, ich, ich,
I could hardly speak.
I thought every German was you.
And the language obscene

An engine, an engine
Chuffing me off like a Jew.
A Jew to Dachau, Auschwitz, Belsen.
I began to talk like a Jew.
I think I may well be a Jew.

The snows of the Tyrol, the clear beer of Vienna
Are not very pure or true.
With my gypsy ancestress and my weird luck
And my Taroc pack and my Taroc pack
I may be a bit of a Jew.

I have always been scared of *you*,
With your Luftwaffe, your gobbledygoo.
And your neat moustache

And your Aryan eye, bright blue.
45   Panzer-man, panzer-man, O You——

Not God but a swastika
So black no sky could squeak through.
Every woman adores a Fascist,
The boot in the face, the brute
50   Brute heart of a brute like you.

You stand at the blackboard, daddy,
In the picture I have of you,
A cleft in your chin instead of your foot
But no less a devil for that, no not
55   Any less the black man who

Bit my pretty red heart in two.
I was ten when they buried you.
At twenty I tried to die
And get back, back, back to you.
60   I thought even the bones would do

But they pulled me out of the sack,
And they stuck me together with glue.
And then I knew what to do.
I made a model of you,
65   A man in black with a Meinkampf look

And a love of the rack and the screw.
And I said I do, I do.
So daddy, I'm finally through.
The black telephone's off at the root,
70   The voices just can't worm through.

If I've killed one man, I've killed two——
The vampire who said he was you
And drank my blood for a year,
Seven years, if you want to know.
75   Daddy, you can lie back now.

There's a stake in your fat black heart
And the villagers never liked you.
They are dancing and stamping on you.
They always *knew* it was you.
Daddy, daddy, you bastard, I'm through.

80

My Papa's Waltz

Theodore Roethke

Theodore Roethke (1908–1963) was born in Saginaw, Michigan. He attended the University of Michigan and Harvard University and taught at Pennsylvania State University, Bennington College, and the University of Washington. His fourth volume of poetry, The Waking *(1953) won the Pulitzer Prize for Poetry and led to his popularity as an American poet.* Words for the Wind *(1958) became his best known work, which included a selection of poems from his previous work. His* Collected Poems *was published posthumously in 1968. "My Papa's Waltz" is the adult son's recollection of, and coming to grips with, the sometimes frenzied behavior of his father.*

The whiskey on your breath
Could make a small boy dizzy;
But I hung on like death:
Such waltzing was not easy.

We romped until the pans
Slid from the kitchen shelf;
My mother's countenance
Could not unfrown itself.

The hand that held my wrist
Was battered on one knuckle;
At every step I missed
My right ear scraped a buckle.

You beat time on my head
With a palm caked hard by dirt,
Then waltzed me off to bed
Still clinging to your shirt.

From *The Collected Poems of Theodore Roethke.* Published by Doubleday, a division of Bantam Doubleday Dell Publishing Group, Inc. Copyright © 1942 by Hearst Magazines, Inc.

Snow White and the Seven Dwarfs

Anne Sexton

Anne Harvey Sexton (1928–1974) was born in Newton, Massachusetts. She married early after a few years of college and soon began both writing poetry and experiencing series of depressions. Her poetry often chronicles her mental instability and often deals with "taboo" female subjects such as incest and adultery. Her first book of poetry, To Bedlam and Part Way Back *(1960) characterizes her worldview and her emotional distress. A later book of poetry,* Live or Die *(1966) won a Pulitzer Prize in 1967. She taught poetry workshops at Boston University in 1970–1971 and at Colgate University in 1971–1972. In 1974 she succumbed to her depression and took her own life. The Snow White poem demonstrates her painful view of personal relationships.*

1 No matter what life you lead
  the virgin is a lovely number:
  cheeks as fragile as cigarette paper,
  arms and legs made of Limoges,
5 lips like Vin Du Rhône,
  rolling her china-blue doll eyes
  open and shut.
  Open to say,
  Good Day Mama,
10 and shut for the thrust
  of the unicorn.

She is unsoiled.
She is as white as a bonefish.

Once there was a lovely virgin
called Snow White.
Say she was thirteen.
Her stepmother,
a beauty in her own right,
though eaten, of course, by age,
would hear of no beauty surpassing her own.
Beauty is a simple passion,
but, oh my friends, in the end
you will dance the fire dance in iron shoes.
The stepmother had a mirror to which she referred—
something like the weather forecast—
a mirror that proclaimed
the one beauty of the land.
She would ask,
Looking glass upon the wall,
who is fairest of us all?
And the mirror would reply,
You are fairest of us all.
Pride pumped in her like poison.

Suddenly one day the mirror replied,
Queen, you are full fair, 'tis true,
but Snow White is fairer than you.
Until that moment Snow White
had been no more important
than a dust mouse under the bed.
But now the queen saw brown spots on her hand
and four whiskers over her lip
so she condemned Snow White
to be hacked to death.
Bring me her heart, she said to the hunter,
and I will salt it and eat it.
The hunter, however, let his prisoner go
and brought a boar's heart back to the castle.
The queen chewed it up like a cube steak.
Now I am fairest, she said,

50   lapping her slim white fingers.   50

Snow White walked in the wildwood
for weeks and weeks.
At each turn there were twenty doorways
and at each stood a hungry wolf,
55   his tongue lolling out like a worm.   55
The birds called out lewdly,
talking like pink parrots,
and the snakes hung down in loops,
each a noose for her sweet white neck.
60   On the seventh week   60
she came to the seventh mountain
and there she found the dwarf house.
It was as droll as a honeymoon cottage
and completely equipped with
65   seven beds, seven chairs, seven forks   65
and seven chamber pots.
Snow White ate seven chicken livers
and lay down, at last, to sleep.

The dwarfs, those little hot dogs,
70   walked three times around Snow White,   70
the sleeping virgin. They were wise
and wattled like small czars.
Yes. It's a good omen,
they said, and will bring us luck.
75   They stood on tiptoes to watch   75
Snow White wake up. She told them
about the mirror and the killer-queen
and they asked her to stay and keep house.
Beware of your stepmother,
80   they said.   80
Soon she will know you are here.
While we are away in the mines
during the day, you must not
open the door.

85   Looking glass upon the wall . . .   85
The mirror told

and so the queen dressed herself in rags
and went out like a peddler to trap Snow White.
She went across seven mountains.
90 She came to the dwarf house
and Snow White opened the door
and bought a bit of lacing.
The queen fastened it tightly
around her bodice,
95 as tight as an Ace bandage,
so tight that Snow White swooned.
She lay on the floor, a plucked daisy.
When the dwarfs came home they undid the lace
and she revived miraculously.
100 She was as full of life as soda pop.
Beware of your stepmother,
they said.
She will try once more.

Looking glass upon the wall . . .
105 Once more the mirror told
and once more the queen dressed in rags
and once more Snow White opened the door.
This time she bought a poison comb,
a curved eight-inch scorpion,
110 and put it in her hair and swooned again.
The dwarfs returned and took out the comb
And she revived miraculously.
She opened her eyes as wide as Orphan Annie.
Beware, beware, they said,
115 but the mirror told,
the queen came,
Snow White, the dumb bunny,
opened the door
and she bit into a poison apple
120 and fell down for the final time.
When the dwarfs returned
they undid her bodice,
they looked for a comb,
but it did no good.

125   Though they washed her with wine   125
         and rubbed her with butter
         it was to no avail.
         She lay as still as a gold piece.

         The seven dwarfs could not bring themselves
130   to bury her in the black ground   130
         so they made a glass coffin
         and set it upon the seventh mountain
         so that all who passed by
         could peek in upon her beauty.
135   A prince came one June day   135
         and would not budge.
         He stayed so long his hair turned green
         and still he would not leave.
         The dwarfs took pity upon him
140   and gave him the glass Snow White—   140
         its doll's eyes shut forever—
         to keep in his far-off castle.
         As the prince's men carried the coffin
         they stumbled and dropped it
145   and the chunk of apple flew out   145
         of her throat and she woke up miraculously.

         And thus Snow White became the prince's bride.
         The wicked queen was invited to the wedding feast
         and when she arrived there were
150   red-hot iron shoes,   150
         in the manner of red-hot roller skates,
         clamped upon her feet.
         First your toes will smoke
         and then your heels will turn black
155   and you will fry upward like a frog,   155
         she was told.
         And so she danced until she was dead,
         a subterranean figure,
         her tongue flicking in and out
160   like a gas jet.   160
         Meanwhile Snow White held court,
         rolling her china-blue doll eyes open and shut

and sometimes referring to her mirror
as women do.

Sonnet 18: Shall I Compare Thee to a Summer's Day?

William Shakespeare

According to tradition, William Shakespeare was born on April 23, 1564 in Stratford-upon-Avon, England. He was the third of eight children born to John and Mary Shakespeare. At age 18, he married 26-year-old Anne Hathaway, six months before the birth of their son. Two years later, there were twins to support as well. It is well known that by the time he was 25, he was a working actor and playwright in London. When he died on his birthday in 1616, he had completed a body of work that ensured his place as the greatest poet and playwright ever to write in English. In addition to writing the nearly forty plays for the stage in London that are best known to the public, Shakespeare wrote a number of poems, including a series (or "cycle") of sonnets that includes the sonnet reprinted here. In it, Shakespeare opens with a rhetorical question, "Shall I compare thee to a summer's day," that represents a conventional kind of flattering overstatement used in love poems of the time.

1 Shall I compare thee to a summer's day?
 Thou art more lovely and more temperate:
 Rough winds do shake the darling buds of May,
 And summer's lease hath all too short a date;
5 Sometime too hot the eye of heaven shines,
 And often is his gold complexion dimmed,
 And every fair from fair sometime declines,
 By chance or nature's changing course untrimmed:
 But thy eternal summer shall not fade,

Shall I Compare Thee To A Summer's Day? (1609)

10   Nor lose possession of that fair thou ow'st,   10
      Nor shall Death brag thou wand'rest in his shade,
      When in eternal lines to time thou grow'st.
          So long as men can breathe or eyes can see,
          So long lives this, and this gives life to thee.

Harrison Bergeron

Kurt Vonnegut Jr.

Kurt Vonnegut (1922–2007) was born in Indianapolis, Indiana. He was educated at Cornell, Carnegie-Mellon, and the University of Chicago, where his master's thesis was unanimously rejected by the department of anthropology. He served in the Army in World War II and was a prisoner of war in Dresden, Germany, during the Allied fire bombing of that city. He worked as a police reporter, a public relations writer, a Saab dealer, and a teacher. Vonnegut was that rarity, a popular writer who also has considerable standing among critics and intellectuals. The novels he wrote during the sixties, especially Cat's Cradle *(1963), found a cult following among students. Slaughterhouse Five (1969), perhaps his best, depicted the destruction by fire-bombing of Dresden. The satire and absurdity that are the trademarks of his novels occur also in "Harrison Bergeron," where Vonnegut sides with the non-conformist, the rule-breaker, the person who stands outside the narrow moral universe of conventional society.*

1   The year was 2081, and everybody was finally equal. They weren't only equal before God and the law. They were equal every which way. Nobody was smarter than anybody else. Nobody was better looking than anybody else. Nobody was stronger or quicker than anybody else. All this equality was due to the 211th, 212th, and 213th Amendments to the Constitution, and to the unceasing vigilance of agents of the United States Handicapper General.

Some things about living still weren't quite right, though. April, for instance, still drove people crazy by not being springtime. And it

Reprinted from *Welcome to the Monkey House* (1961), by permission of Bantam Dell Publishing, a division of Random House, Inc.

was in that clammy month that the H-G men took George and Hazel Bergeron's fourteen-year-old son, Harrison, away.

It was tragic, all right, but George and Hazel couldn't think about it very hard. Hazel had a perfectly average intelligence, which meant she couldn't think about anything except in short bursts. And George, while his intelligence was way above normal, had a little mental handicap radio in his ear. He was required by law to wear it at all times. It was tuned to a government transmitter. Every twenty seconds or so, the transmitter would send out some sharp noise to keep people like George from taking unfair advantage of their brains.

George and Hazel were watching television. There were tears on Hazel's cheeks, but she'd forgotten for the moment what they were about.

5   On the television screen were ballerinas.   5

A buzzer sounded in George's head. His thoughts fled in panic, like bandits from a burglar alarm.

"That was a real pretty dance, that dance they just did," said Hazel.

"Huh?" said George.

"That dance—it was nice," said Hazel.

10   "Yup," said George. He tried to think a little about the ballerinas. 10 They weren't really very good—no better than anybody else would have been, anyway. They were burdened with sashweights and bags of birdshot, and their faces were masked, so that no one, seeing a free and graceful gesture or a pretty face, would feel like something the cat drug in. George was toying with the vague notion that maybe dancers shouldn't be handicapped. But he didn't get very far with it before another noise in his ear radio scattered his thoughts.

George winced. So did two out of the eight ballerinas.

Hazel saw him wince. Having no mental handicap herself, she had to ask George what the latest sound had been.

"Sounded like somebody hitting a milk bottle with a ball peen hammer," said George

"I'd think it would be real interesting, hearing all the different sounds," said Hazel, a little envious. "All the things they think up."

15   "Um," said George.   15

"Only, if I was Handicapper General, you know what I would do?" said Hazel. Hazel, as a matter of fact, bore a strong resemblance to the Handicapper General, a woman named Diana Moon Glampers. "If I was Diana Moon Glampers," said Hazel, "I'd have chimes on Sunday—just chimes. Kind of in honor of religion."

"I could think, if it was just chimes," said George.

"Well—maybe make 'em real loud," said Hazel. "I think I'd make a good Handicapper General."

"Good as anybody else," said George.

20 "Who knows better'n I do what normal is?" said Hazel.   20

"Right," said George. He began to think glimmeringly about his abnormal son who was now in jail, about Harrison, but a twenty-one-gun salute in his head stopped that.

"Boy!" said Hazel, "that was a doozy, wasn't it?"

It was such a doozy that George was white and trembling, and tears stood on the rims of his red eyes. Two of the eight ballerinas had collapsed to the studio floor, [and] were holding their temples.

"All of a sudden you look so tired," said Hazel. "Why don't you stretch out on the sofa, so's you can rest your handicap bag on the pillows, honeybunch." She was referring to the forty-seven pounds of birdshot in a canvas bag, which was padlocked around George's neck. "Go on and rest the bag for a little while," she said. "I don't care if you're not equal to me for a while."

25 George weighed the bag with his hands. "I don't mind it," he   25
said. "I don't notice it any more. It's just a part of me."

"You been so tired lately—kind of wore out," said Hazel. "if there was just some way we could make a little hole in the bottom of the bag, and just take out a few of them lead balls. Just a few."

"Two years in prison and two thousand dollars fine for every ball I took out," said George. "I don't call that a bargain."

"If you could just take a few out when you came home from work," said Hazel. "I mean—you don't compete with anybody around here. You just set around."

"If I tried to get away with it," said George, "then other people'd get away with it—and pretty soon we'd be right back to the dark ages again, with everybody competing against everybody else. You wouldn't like that, would you?"

30 "I'd hate it," said Hazel.   30

"There you are," said George. "The minute people start cheating on laws, what do you think happens to society?"

If Hazel hadn't been able to come up with an answer to this question George couldn't have supplied one. A siren was going off in his head.

"Reckon it'd fall all apart," said Hazel.

"What would?" said George blankly.

35   "Society," said Hazel uncertainly. "Wasn't that what you just   35
said?"

"Who knows?" said George.

The television program was suddenly interrupted for a news bulletin. It wasn't clear at first as to what the bulletin was about, since the announcer, like all announcers, had a serious speech impediment. For about half a minute, and in a state of high excitement, the announcer tried to say, "Ladies and gentlemen—"

He finally gave up, handed the bulletin to a ballerina to read.

"That's all right—" Hazel said of the announcer, "he tried. That's the big thing. He tried to do the best he could with what God gave him. He should get a nice raise for trying so hard."

40   "Ladies and gentlemen—" said the ballerina, reading the bulletin.   40
She must have been extraordinarily beautiful, because the mask she wore was hideous. And it was easy to see that she was the strongest and most graceful of all the dancers, for her handicap bags were as big as those worn by two-hundred-pound men.

And she had to apologize at once for her voice, which was a very unfair voice for a woman to use. Her voice was a warm, luminous, timeless melody. "Excuse me—" she said, and she began again, making her voice absolutely uncompetitive.

"Harrison Bergeron, age fourteen," she said in a grackle squawk, "has just escaped from jail, where he was held on suspicion of plotting to overthrow the government. He is a genius and an athlete, is under-handicapped, and should be regarded as extremely dangerous."

A police photograph of Harrison Bergeron was flashed on the screen upside down, then sideways, upside down again, then right side up. The picture showed the full length of Harrison against a background calibrated in feet and inches. He was exactly seven feet tall.

The rest of Harrison's appearance was Halloween and hardware. Nobody had ever borne heavier handicaps. He had outgrown hindrances faster than the H-G men could think them up. Instead of a little ear radio for a mental handicap, he wore a tremendous pair of earphones, and spectacles with thick wavy lenses. The spectacles were intended to make him not only half blind, but to give him whanging headaches besides.

45   Scrap metal was hung all over him. Ordinarily, there was a certain   45
symmetry, a military neatness to the handicaps issued to strong people, but Harrison looked like a walking junkyard. In the race of life, Harrison carried three hundred pounds.

And to offset his good looks, the H-G men required that he wear at all times a red rubber ball for a nose, keep his eyebrows shaved off, and cover his even white teeth with black caps at snaggle-tooth random.

"If you see this boy," said the ballerina, "do not—I repeat, do not—try to reason with him."

There was the shriek of a door being torn from its hinges.

Screams and barking cries of consternation came from the television set. The photograph of Harrison Bergeron on the screen jumped again and again, as though dancing to the tune of an earthquake.

50 George Bergeron correctly identified the earthquake, and well he might have—for many was the time his own home had danced to the same crashing tune. "My God—" said George, "that must be Harrison!"

The realization was blasted from his mind instantly by the sound of an automobile collision in his head.

When George could open his eyes again, the photograph of Harrison was gone. A living, breathing Harrison filled the screen.

Clanking, clownish, and huge, Harrison stood in the center of the studio. The knob of the uprooted studio door was still in his hand. Ballerinas, technicians, musicians, and announcers cowered on their knees before him, expecting to die.

"I am the Emperor!" cried Harrison. "Do you hear? I am the Emperor! Everybody must do what I say at once!" He stamped his foot and the studio shook.

55 "Even as I stand here—-" he bellowed, "crippled, hobbled, sickened—I am a greater ruler than any man who ever lived. Now watch me become what I *can* become!"

Harrison tore the straps of his handicap harness like wet tissue paper, tore straps guaranteed to support five thousand pounds.

Harrison's scrap-iron handicaps crashed to the floor.

Harrison thrust his thumbs under the bar of the padlock that secured his head harness. The bar snapped like celery. Harrison smashed his headphones and spectacles against the wall.

He flung away his rubber-ball nose, revealed a man that would have awed Thor, the god of thunder.

60 "I shall now select my Empress!" he said, looking down on the cowering people. "Let the first woman who dares rise to her feet claim her mate and her throne!"

A moment passed, and then a ballerina arose swaying like a willow.

Harrison plucked the mental handicap from her ear, snapped off her physical handicaps with marvelous delicacy. Last of all, he removed her mask.

She was blindingly beautiful.

"Now—" said Harrison, taking her hand, "shall we show the people the meaning of the word dance? Music!" he commanded.

65 The musicians scrambled back into their chairs, and Harrison stripped them of their handicaps, too. "Play your best," he told them, "and I'll make you barons and dukes and earls."

The music began. It was normal at first—cheap, silly, false. But Harrison snatched two musicians from their chairs, waved them like batons as he sang the music as he wanted it played. He slammed them back into their chairs.

The music began again and was much improved.

Harrison and his Empress merely listened to the music for a while—listened gravely, as though synchronizing their heartbeats with it.

They shifted their weights to their toes.

70 Harrison placed his big hands on the girl's tiny waist, letting her sense the weightlessness that would soon be hers.

And then, in an explosion of joy and grace, into the air they sprang!

Not only were the laws of the land abandoned, but the law of gravity and the laws of motion as well.

They reeled, whirled, swiveled, flounced, capered, gamboled, and spun.

They leaped like deer on the moon.

75 The studio ceiling was thirty feet high, but each leap brought the dancers nearer to it.

It became their obvious intention to kiss the ceiling.

They kissed it.

And then, neutralizing gravity with love and pure will, they remained suspended in air inches below the ceiling, and they kissed each other for a long, long time.

It was then that Diana Moon Glampers, the Handicapper General, came into the studio with a double-barreled ten-gauge shotgun. She fired twice and the Emperor and the Empress were dead before they hit the floor.

80   Diana Moon Glampers loaded the gun again. She aimed it at the 80
musicians and told them they had ten seconds to get their handicaps
back on.

   It was then that the Bergerons' television tube burned out. Hazel
turned to comment about the blackout to George. But George had
gone out into the kitchen for a can of beer.

   George came back in with the beer, paused while a handicap signal shook him up. And then he sat down again.

   "You been crying?" he said to Hazel.

   "Yup," she said.

85   "What about?" he said. 85

   "I forget," she said. "Something real sad on television."

   "What was it?" he said.

   "It's all kind of mixed up in my mind," said Hazel.

   "Forget sad things," said George.

90   "I always do," said Hazel. 90

   "That's my girl," said George. He winced. There was the sound
of a riveting gun in his head.

   "Gee— I could tell that one was a doozy," said Hazel.

   "You can say that again," said George.

   "Gee—" said Hazel, "I could tell that one was a doozy."

Everyday Use

Alice Walker

Alice Walker (1944–) was born in Georgia to sharecropper parents. She attended Spelman College and Sarah Lawrence College and was active in the civil rights movement of the 1960s. Publishing her first novel, The Third Life of Grange Copeland, *at the age of 26, she has been a prolific writer since. In all, she has published five novels, two short story collections, two collections of essays, and several books of poems. Her novel* The Color Purple *(1982) is perhaps her best known, having won the American Book Award, the Pulitzer Prize, and the Candace Award of the National Coalition of 100 Black Women. The novel was also made into a prize-winning film by director Steven Spielberg. Walker's topics run the gamut of human experience and include some harsh realities such as incest and racial violence as well as relationships within families and society. "Everyday Use" is a short story published in* In Love and Trouble *(1973). In it Walker deals with a number of themes common in her work: changes between generations, family tensions, African-American heritage. You should notice right away that in this story Walker is writing from the point of view of a woman other than herself.*

for your grandmama

1   I will wait for her in the yard that Maggie and I made so clean and   1
wavy yesterday afternoon. A yard like this is more comfortable than most people know. It is not just a yard. It is like an extended living room. When the hard clay is swept clean as a floor and the fine sand around the edges lined with tiny, irregular grooves, anyone can

come and sit and look up into the elm tree and wait for the breezes that never come inside the house.

Maggie will be nervous until after her sister goes: she will stand hopelessly in corners, homely and ashamed of the burn scars down her arms and legs, eying her sister with a mixture of envy and awe. She thinks her sister has held life always in the palm of one hand, that "no" is a word the world never learned to say to her.

You've no doubt seen those TV shows where the child who has "made it" is confronted, as a surprise, by her own mother and father, tottering in weakly from backstage. (A pleasant surprise, of course: What would they do if parent and child came on the show only to curse out and insult each other?) On TV mother and child embrace and smile into each other's faces. Sometimes the mother and father weep, the child wraps them in her arms and leans across the table to tell how she would not have made it without their help, I have seen these programs.

Sometimes I dream a dream in which Dee and I are suddenly brought together on a TV program of this sort. Out of a dark and soft-seated limousine I am ushered into to a bright room filled with many people. There I meet a smiling, gray, sporty man like Johnny Carson who shakes my hand and tells me what a fine girl I have. Then we are on the stage and Dee is embracing me with tears in her eyes. She pins on my dress a large orchid, even though she has told me once that she thinks orchids are tacky flowers.

5   In real life I am a large, big-boned woman with rough, man-working hands. In the winter I wear flannel nightgowns to bed and overalls during the day. I can kill and clean a hog as mercilessly as a man. My fat keeps me hot in zero weather. I can work outside all day, breaking ice to get water for washing; I can eat pork liver cooked over the open fire minutes after it comes steaming from the hog. One winter I knocked a bull calf straight in the brain between the eyes with a sledge hammer and had the meat hung up to chill before nightfall. But of course all this does not show on television. I am the way my daughter would want me to be: a hundred pounds lighter, my skin like an uncooked barley pancake. My hair glistens in the hot bright lights. Johnny Carson has much to do to keep up with my quick and witty tongue.

But that is a mistake. I know even before I wake up. Who ever knew a Johnson with a quick tongue? Who can even imagine me looking a strange white man in the eye? It seems to me I have talked to them always with one foot raised in flight, with my head turned in whichever way is farthest from them. Dee, though. She would always look anyone in the eye. Hesitation was no part of her nature.

"How do I look, Mama?" Maggie says, showing just enough of her thin body enveloped in pink skirt and red blouse for me to know she's there, almost hidden by the door.

"Come out into the yard," I say.

Have you ever seen a lame animal, perhaps a dog run over by some careless person rich enough to own a car, sidle up to someone who is ignorant enough to be kind to him? That is the way my Maggie walks. She has been like this, chin on chest, eyes on ground, feet in shuffle, ever since the fire that burned the other house to the ground.

10 Dee is lighter than Maggie, with nicer hair and a fuller figure. 10 She's a woman now, though sometimes I forget. How long ago was it that the other house burned? Ten, twelve years? Sometimes I can still hear the flames and feel Maggie's arms sticking to me, her hair smoking and her dress falling off her in little black papery flakes. Her eyes seemed stretched open, blazed open by the flames reflected in them. And Dee. I see her standing off under the sweet gum tree she used to dig gum out of, a look of concentration on her face as she watched the last dingy gray board of the house fall in toward the red-hot brick chimney. Why don't you do a dance around the ashes? I'd wanted to ask her. She had hated the house that much.

I used to think she hated Maggie, too. But that was before we raised the money, the church and me, to send her to Augusta to school. She used to read to us without pity; forcing words, lies, other folks' habits, whole lives upon us two, sitting trapped and ignorant underneath her voice. She washed us in a river of make-believe, burned us with a lot of knowledge we didn't necessarily need to know. Pressed us to her with the serious way she read, to shove us away at just the moment, like dimwits, we seemed about to understand.

Dee wanted nice things. A yellow organdy dress to wear to her graduation from high school; black pumps to match a green suit she'd made from an old suit somebody gave me. She was determined to stare down any disaster in her efforts. Her eyelids would not flicker for minutes at a time. Often I fought off the temptation to shake her. At sixteen she had a style of her own: and knew what style was.

I never had an education myself. After second grade the school was closed down. Don't ask me why: in 1927 colored asked fewer questions than they do now. Sometimes Maggie reads to me. She stumbles along good-naturedly but can't see well. She knows she is not bright. Like good looks and money, quickness passed her by. She will marry John Thomas (who has mossy teeth in an earnest face) and then I'll be free to sit here and I guess just sing church songs to myself. Although I never was a good singer. Never could carry a tune. I was always better at a man's job. I used to love to milk till I was hooked in the side in '49. Cows are soothing and slow and don't bother you, unless you try to milk them the wrong way.

I have deliberately turned my back on the house. It is three rooms, just like the one that burned, except the roof is tin; they don't make shingle roofs any more. There are no real windows, just some holes cut in the sides, like the portholes in a ship, but not round and not square, with rawhide holding the shutters up on the outside. This house is in a pasture, too, like the other one. No doubt when Dee sees it she will want to tear it down. She wrote me once that no matter where we "choose" to live, she will manage to come see us. But she will never bring her friends. Maggie and I thought about this and Maggie asked me, "Mama, when did Dee ever *have* any friends?"

15 She had a few. Furtive boys in pink shirts banging about on wash- 15 day after school. Nervous girls who never laughed. Impressed with her they worshiped the well-turned phrase, the cute shape, the scalding humor that erupted like bubbles in lye. She read to them.

When she was courting Jimmy T she didn't have much time to pay to us, but turned all her faultfinding power on him. He *flew* to marry a cheap city girl from a family of ignorant flashy people. She hardly had time to recompose herself.

When she comes I will meet—but there they are!

Maggie attempts to make a dash for the house, in her shuffling way, but I stay her with my hand. "Come back here," I say. And she stops and tries to dig a well in the sand with her toe.

It is hard to see them clearly through the strong sun. But even the first glimpse of leg out of the car tells me it is Dee. Her feet were always neat-looking, as if God himself had shaped them with a certain style. From the other side of the car comes a short, stocky man. Hair is all over his head a foot long and hanging from his chin like a kinky mule tail. I hear Maggie suck in her breath. "Uhnnnh," is what it sounds like. Like when you see the wriggling end of a snake just in front of your foot on the road. "Uhnnnh."

20 Dee next. A dress down to the ground, in this hot weather. A 20 dress so loud it hurts my eyes. There are yellows and oranges enough to throw back the light of the sun. I feel my whole face warming from the heat waves it throws out. Earrings gold, too, and hanging down to her shoulders. Bracelets dangling and making noises when she moves her arm up to shake the folds of the dress out of her armpits. The dress is loose and flows, and as she walks closer, I like it. I hear Maggie go "Uhnnnh" again. It is her sister's hair. It stands straight up like the wool on a sheep. It is black as night and around the edges are two long pigtails that rope about like small lizards disappearing behind her ears.

"Wa-su-zo-Tean-o!" she says, coming on in that gliding way the dress makes her move. The short stocky fellow with the hair to his navel is all grinning and he follows up with "Asalamalakim, my mother and sister!" He moves to hug Maggie but she falls back, right up against the back of my chair. I feel her trembling there and when I look up I see the perspiration falling off her chin.

"Don't get up," says Dee. Since I am stout it takes something of a push. You can see me trying to move a second or two before I make it. She turns, showing white heels through her sandals, and goes back to the car. Out she peeks next with a Polaroid. She stoops down quickly and lines up picture after picture of me sitting there in front of the house with Maggie cowering behind me. She never takes a shot without making sure the house is included. When a cow comes nibbling around the edge of the yard she snaps it and me and Maggie *and* the house. Then she puts the Polaroid in the back seat of the car, and comes up and kisses me on the forehead.

Meanwhile Asalamalakim is going through motions with Maggie's hand. Maggie's hand is as limp as a fish, and probably as cold, despite the sweat, and she keeps trying to pull it back. It looks like Asalamalakim wants to shake hands but wants to do it fancy. Or maybe be don't know how people shake hands. Anyhow, he soon gives up on Maggie.

"Well," I say. "Dee."

25 "No, Mama," she says. "Not 'Dee,' Wangero Leewanika Kemanjo!" 25
"What happened to 'Dee'?" I wanted to know.

"She's dead," Wangero said. "I couldn't bear it any longer, being named after the people who oppress me."

"You know as well as me you was named after your aunt Dicie," I said. Dicie is my sister. She named Dee. We called her "Big Dee" after Dee was born.

"But who was she named after?" asked Wangero.

30 "I guess after Grandma Dee," I said.

"And who was she named after?" asked Wangero.

"Her mother," I said, and saw Wangero was getting tired. "That's about as far back as I can trace it," I said. Though, in fact, I probably could have carried it back beyond the Civil War through the branches.

"Well," said Asalamalakim, "there you are."

"Uhnnnh," I heard Maggie say.

35 "There I was not," I said, "before 'Dicie' cropped up in our family, so why should I try to trace it that far back?"

He just stood there grinning, looking down on me like somebody inspecting a Model A car. Every once in a while he and Wangero sent eye signals over my head.

"How do you pronounce this name?" I asked.

"You don't have to call me by it if you don't want to," said Wangero.

"Why shouldn't I?" I asked. "If that's what you want us to call you, we'll call you."

40 "I know it might sound awkward at first," said Wangero.

"I'll get used to it," I said. "Ream it out again."

Well, soon we got the name out of the way. Asalamalakim had a name twice as long and three times as hard. After I tripped over it two or three times he told me to just call him Hakim-a-barber. I wanted to ask him was he a barber, but I didn't really think he was, so I didn't ask.

"You must belong to those beef-cattle peoples down the road," I said. They said "Asalamalakim" when they met you, too, but they didn't shake hands. Always too busy: feeding the cattle, fixing the fences, putting up salt-lick shelters, throwing down hay. When the white folks poisoned some of the herd the men stayed up all night with rifles in their hands. I walked a mile and a half just to see the sight.

Hakim-a-barber said, "I accept some of their doctrines, but farming and raising cattle is not my style." (They didn't tell me, and I didn't ask, whether Wangero [Dee] had really gone and married him.)

45   We sat down to eat and right away he said he didn't eat collards   45
and pork was unclean. Wangero, though, went on through the chitlins
and corn bread, the greens and everything else. She talked a blue streak
over the sweet potatoes. Everything delighted her. Even the fact that
we still used the benches her daddy made for the table when we
couldn't afford to buy chairs.

"Oh, Mama!" she cried. Then turned to Hakim-a-barber. "I never
knew how lovely these benches are. You can feel the rump prints," she
said, running her hands underneath her and along the bench. Then
she gave a sigh and her hand closed over Grandma Dee's butter dish.
"That's it!" she said. "I knew there was something I wanted to ask you
if I could have." She jumped up from the table and went over in the
corner where the churn stood, the milk in it clabber by now. She
looked at the churn and looked at it.

"This churn top is what I need," she said. "Didn't Uncle Buddy
whittle it out of a tree you all used to have?"

"Yes," I said.

"Uh huh," she said happily. "And I want the dasher, too."

50   "Uncle Buddy whittle that, too?" asked the barber.   50

Dee (Wangero) looked up at me.

"Aunt Dee's first husband whittled the dash," said Maggie so low
you almost couldn't hear her. "His name was Henry, but they called
him Stash."

"Maggie's brain is like an elephant's," Wangero said, laughing. "I
can use the churn top as a centerpiece for the alcove table," she said,
sliding a plate over the churn, "and I'll think of something artistic to
do with the dasher."

When she finished wrapping the dasher the handle stuck out. I
took it for a moment in my hands. You didn't even have to look close
to see where hands pushing the dasher up and down to make butter
had left a kind of sink in the wood. In fact, there were a lot of small
sinks; you could see where thumbs and fingers had sunk into the
wood. It was beautiful light yellow wood, from a tree that grew in the
yard where Big Dee and Stash had lived.

55   After dinner Dee (Wangero) went to the trunk at the foot of my   55
bed and started rifling through it. Maggie hung back in the kitchen
over the dishpan. Out came Wangero with two quilts. They had been
pieced by Grandma Dee and then Big Dee and me had hung them on
the quilt frames on the front porch and quilted them. One was in the

172

Lone Star pattern. The other was Walk Around the Mountain. In both of them were scraps of dresses Grandma Dee had worn fifty and more years ago. Bits and pieces of Granpa Jarrell's Paisley shirts. And one teeny faded blue piece, about the size of a penny matchbox, that was from Great Grandpa' Ezra's uniform that he wore in the Civil War.

"Mama," Wangero said sweet as a bird. "Can I have these old quilts?"

I heard something fall in the kitchen, and a minute later the kitchen door slammed.

"Why don't you take one or two of the others?" I asked. "These old things was just done by me and Big Dee from some tops your grandma pieced before she died."

"No," said Wangero. "I don't want those. They are stitched around the borders by machine."

60 "That'll make them last better," I said 60

"That's not the point," said Wangero. "These are all pieces of dresses Grandma used to wear. She did all this stitching by hand. Imagine!" She held the quilts securely in her arms, stroking them.

"Some of the pieces, like those lavender ones, come from old clothes her mother handed down to her," I said, moving up to touch the quilts. Dee (Wangero) moved back just enough so that I couldn't reach the quilts. They already belonged to her.

"Imagine!" she breathed again, clutching them closely to her bosom.

"The truth is," I said. "I promised to give them quilts to Maggie, for when she marries John Thomas."

65 She gasped like a bee had stung her. 65

"Maggie can't appreciate these quilts!" she said. "She'd probably be backward enough to put them to everyday use."

"I reckon she would," I said. "God knows I been saving 'em for long enough with nobody using 'em. I hope she will!" I didn't want to bring up how I had offered Dee (Wangero) a quilt when she went away to college. Then she had told me they were old-fashioned, out of style.

"But they're *priceless!*" she was saying now, furiously; for she has a temper. "Maggie would put them on the bed and in five years they'd be in rags. Less than that!"

"She can always make some more," I said. "Maggie knows how to quilt."

70 Dee (Wangero) looked at me with hatred. "You just will not un- 70
derstand. The point is these quilts, *these* quilts!"

"Well," I said, stumped. "What would *you* do with them?"

"Hang them," she said. As if that was the only thing you *could* do
with quilts.

Maggie by now was standing in the door. I could almost hear the
sound her feet made as they scraped over each other.

"She can have them, Mama," she said, like somebody used to
never winning anything, or having anything reserved for her. "I can
'member Grandma Dee without the quilts."

75 I looked at her hard. She had filled her bottom lip with checker- 75
berry snuff and it gave her face a kind of dopey, hangdog look. It was
Grandma Dee and big Dee who taught her how to quilt herself. She
stood there with her scarred hands hidden in the folds of her skirt. She
looked at her sister with something like fear but she wasn't mad at her.
This was Maggie's portion. This was the way she knew God to work.

When I looked at her like that something hit me in the top of my
head and ran down to the soles of my feet. Just like when I'm in
church and the spirit of God touches me and I get happy and shout.
I did something I never had done before: hugged Maggie to me, then
dragged her on into the room, snatched the quilts out of Miss
Wangero's hands and dumped them into Maggie's lap. Maggie just sat
there on my bed with her mouth open.

"Take one or two of the others," I said to Dee.

But she turned without a word and went out to Hakim-a-barber.

"You just don't understand," she said, as Maggie and I came out
to the car.

80 "What don't I understand?" I wanted to know. 80

"Your heritage," she said. And then she turned to Maggie, kissed
her, and said, "You ought to try to make something of yourself, too,
Maggie. It's really a new day for us. But from the way you and Mama
still live you'd never know it."

She put on some sunglasses that hid everything above the tip of
her nose and her chin.

Maggie smiled; maybe at the sunglasses. But a real smile, not
scared. After we watched the car dust settle I asked Maggie to bring
me a dip of snuff. And then the two of us sat there just enjoying, until
it was time to go in the house and go to bed.

A Worn Path

Eudora Welty

*Born in Jackson, Mississippi, Eudora Welty (1909-) at-
tended Mississippi State College for Women and was graduated from the University of Wisconsin in 1929. She lived
briefly in New York, where she worked in an advertising
firm, but returned to her native Mississippi during the
Great Depression to help her family and to write. Welty has
published three novels and many stories and articles; she
won the O. Henry short fiction award, the Pulitzer Prize
for her novel* The Optimist's Daughter *(1972), the National Medal for Literature, and the Presidential Medal of
Freedom, thus becoming one of the most honored and admired writers of the century. Welty captures the life of the
South and the lives of the people she knew and loved. That
tenderness is clearly demonstrated in "A Worn Path."*

1   It was December—a bright frozen day in the early morning. Far   1
out in the country there was an old Negro woman with her head
tied in a red rag, coming along a path through the pinewoods. Her
name was Phoenix Jackson. She was very old and small and she
walked, slowly in the dark pine shadows, moving a little from side to
side in her steps, with the balanced heaviness and lightness of a pen-
dulum in a grandfather clock. She carried a thin, small cane made
from an umbrella, and with this she kept tapping the frozen earth in
front of her. This made a grave and persistent noise in the still air, that
seemed meditative, like the chirping of a solitary little bird.

   She wore a dark striped dress reaching down to her shoetops, and
an equally long apron of bleached sugar sacks, with a full pocket; all,
neat and tidy, but every time she took a step she might have fallen over

her shoelaces, which dragged from her unlaced shoes. She looked straight ahead. Her eyes were blue with age. Her skin had a pattern all its own of numberless branching wrinkles and as though a whole little tree stood in the middle of her forehead, but a golden color ran underneath, and the two knobs of her cheeks were illuminated by a yellow burning under the dark. Under the red rag her hair came down on her neck in the frailest of ringlets, still black, and with an odor like copper.

Now and then there was a quivering in the thicket. Old Phoenix said, "Out of my way, all you foxes, owls, beetles, jack rabbits, coons, and wild animals! . . . Keep out from under these feet, little bobwhites. . . . Keep the big wild hogs out of my path. Don't let none of those come running in my direction. I got a long way." Under her small black-freckled hand her cane, limber as a buggy whip, would switch at the brush as if to rouse up any hiding things.

On she went. The woods were deep and still. The sun made the pine needles almost too bright to look at, up where the wind rocked. The cones dropped as light as feathers. Down in the hollow was the mourning dove—it was not too late for him.

5   The path ran up a hill. "Seem like there is chains about my feet,   5
time I get this far," she said, in the voice of argument old people keep to use with themselves. "Something always take a hold on this hill— pleads I should stay."

After she got to the top she turned and gave a full, severe look behind her where she had come. "Up through pines," she said at length. "Now down through oaks."

Her eyes opened their widest and she started down gently. But before she got to the bottom of the hill a bush caught her dress.

Her fingers were busy and intent, but her skirts were full and long, so that before she could pull them free in one place they were caught in another. It was not possible to allow the dress to tear. "I in the thorny bush," she said. "Thorns, you doing your appointed work. Never want to let folks past—no sir. Old eyes thought you was a pretty little *green* bush."

Finally, trembling all over, she stood free, and after a moment dared to stoop for her cane.

10   "Sun so high!" she cried, leaning back and looking, while the   10
thick tears went over her eyes. "The time getting all gone here."

At the foot of this hill was a place where a log was laid across the creek.

"Now comes the trial," said Phoenix.

Putting her right foot out, she mounted the log and shut her eyes. Lifting her skirt, leveling her cane fiercely before her, like a festival figure in some parade, she began to march across. Then she opened her eyes and she was safe on the other side.

"I wasn't as old as I thought," she said.

15 But she sat down to rest. She spread her skirts on the bank around 15
her and folded her hands over her knees. Up above her was a tree in a pearly cloud of mistletoe. She did not dare to close her eyes, and when a little boy brought her a little plate with a slice of marble-cake on it she spoke to him. "That would be acceptable," she said. But when she went to take it there was just her own hand in the air.

So she left that tree, and had to go through a barbed-wire fence. There she had to creep and crawl, spreading her knees and stretching her fingers like a baby trying to climb the steps. But she talked loudly to herself: she could not let her dress be torn now, so late in the day, and she could not pay for having her arm or leg sawed off if she got caught fast where she was.

At last she was safe through the fence and risen up out in the clearing. Big dead trees, like black men with one arm, were standing in the purple stalks of the withered cotton field. There sat a buzzard.

"Who you watching?"

In the furrow she made her way along

20 "Glad this not the season for bulls," she said, looking sideways, 20
"and the good Lord made his snakes to curl up and sleep in the winter. A pleasure I don't see no two-headed snake coming around that tree, where it come once. It took a while to get by him, back in the summer."

She passed through the old cotton and went into a field of dead corn. It whispered and shook, and was taller than her head. "Through the maze now," she said, for there was no path.

Then there was something tall, black, and skinny there, moving before her.

At first she took it for a man. It could have been a man dancing in the field. But she stood still and listened, and it did not make a sound. It was as silent as a ghost.

"Ghost," she said sharply, "who be you the ghost of? For I have heard of nary death close by."

But there was no answer, only the ragged dancing in the wind.

She shut her eyes, reached out her hand, and touched a sleeve. She found a coat and inside that an emptiness, cold as ice.

"You scarecrow," she said. Her face lighted. "I ought to be shut up for good," she said with laughter. "My senses is gone. I too old. I the oldest people I ever know. Dance, old scarecrow," she said, "while I dancing with you."

She kicked her foot over the furrow, and with mouth drawn down shook her head once or twice in a little strutting way. Some husks blew down and whirled in streamers about her skirts.

Then she went on, parting her way from side to side with the cane, through the whispering field. At last she came to the end, to a wagon track, where the silver grass blew between the red ruts. The quail were walking around like pullets, seeming all dainty and unseen.

"Walk pretty," she said. "This the easy place. This the easy going."

She followed the track, swaying through the quiet bare fields, through the little strings of trees silver in their dead leaves, past cabins silver from weather, with the doors and windows boarded shut, all like old women under a spell sitting there. "I walking in their sleep," she said, nodding her head vigorously.

In a ravine she went where a spring was silently flowing through a hollow log. Old Phoenix bent and drank. "Sweetgum makes the water sweet," she said, and drank more. "Nobody knows who made this well, for it was here when I was born."

The track crossed a swampy part where the moss hung as white as lace from every limb. "Sleep on, alligators, and blow your bubbles." Then the track went into the road.

Deep, deep the road went down between the high green-colored banks. Overhead the live-oaks met, and it was as dark as a cave.

A black dog with a lolling tongue came up out of the weeds by the ditch. She was meditating, and not ready, and when he came at her she only hit him a little with her cane. Over she went in the ditch, like a little puff of milk-weed.

Down there, her senses drifted away. A dream visited her, and she reached her hand up, but nothing reached down and gave her a pull. So she lay there and presently went to talking. "Old woman," she said to herself, "that black dog come up out of the weeds to stall you off, and now there he sitting on his fine tail, smiling at you."

A white man finally came along and found her—a hunter, a young man, with his dog on a chain.

"Well, Granny!" he laughed. "What are you doing there?"

"Lying on my back like a June-bug waiting to be turned over, mister," she said, reaching up her hand.

He lifted her up, gave her a swing in the air, and set her down. "Anything broken, Granny?"

"No, sir, them old dead weeds is springy enough," said Phoenix, when she had got her breath. "I thank you for your trouble."

"Where do you live, Granny?" he asked, while the two dogs were growling at each other.

"Away back yonder, sir, behind that ridge. You can't even see it from here."

"On your way home?"

"No, sir, I going to town."

"Why that's too far! That's as far as I walk when I come out myself, and I get something for my trouble." He patted the stuffed bag he carried, and there hung down a little closed claw. It was one of the bobwhites, with its beak hooked bitterly to show it was dead. "Now you go on home, Granny!"

"I bound to go to town, mister," said Phoenix. "The time come around."

He gave another laugh, filling the whole landscape. "I know you colored people! Wouldn't miss going to town to see Santa Claus!"

But something held Old Phoenix very still. The deep lines in her face went into a fierce and different radiation. Without warning she had seen with her own eyes a flashing nickel fall out of the man's pocket on to the ground.

"How old are you, Granny?" he was saying.

"There is no telling, mister," she said, "no telling."

Then she gave a little cry and clapped her hands, and said, "Git on away from here, dog! Look! Look at that dog!" She laughed as if in admiration. "He ain't scared of nobody. He a big black dog." She whispered, "Sick him!"

"Watch me get rid of that cur," said the man. "Sick him, Pete! Sick him!"

Phoenix heard the dogs fighting and heard the man running and throwing sticks. She even heard a gunshot. But she was slowly bending forward by that time, further and further forward, the lids stretched down over her eyes, as if she were doing this in her sleep. Her chin was lowered almost to her knees. The yellow palm of her hand came out from the fold of her apron. Her fingers slid down and along the ground under the piece of money with the grace and care they would have in lifting an egg from under a sitting hen. Then she slowly straightened up, she stood erect, and the nickel was in her apron pocket. A bird flew by. Her lips moved. "God watching me the whole time. I come to stealing."

55   The man came back, and his own dog panted about them. "Well,   55
I scared him off that time," he said, and then he laughed and lifted his gun and pointed it at Phoenix.

She stood straight and faced him.

"Doesn't the gun scare you?" he said, still pointing it.

"No, sir, I seen plenty go off closer by, in my day, and for less what I done," she said, holding utterly still.

He smiled, and shouldered the gun. "Well, Granny," he said, "you must be a hundred years old, and scared of nothing. I'd give you a dime if I had any money with me. But you take my advice and stay home, and nothing will happen to you."

60   "I bound to go on my way, mister," said Phoenix. She inclined her   60
head in the red rag. Then they went in different directions, but she could hear the gun shooting again and again over the hill.

She walked on. The shadows hung from the oak trees to the road like curtains. Then she smelled wood-smoke, and smelled the river, and she saw a steeple and the cabins on their steep steps. Dozens of little black children whirled around her. There ahead was Natchez shining. Bells were ringing. She walked on.

In the paved city it was Christmas time. There were red and green electric lights strung and crisscrossed everywhere, and all turned on in the daytime. Old Phoenix would have been lost if she had not distrusted her eyesight and depended on her feet to know where to take her.

She paused quietly on the sidewalk, where people were passing by. A lady came along in the crowd, carrying an armful of red-, green-, and silver-wrapped presents; she gave off perfume like the red roses in hot summer, and Phoenix stopped her.

"Please, missy, will you lace up my shoe?" She held up her foot.

65 "What do you want, Grandma?"

"See my shoe," said Phoenix. "Do all right for out in the country, but wouldn't look right to go in a big building."

"Stand still then, Grandma," said the lady. She put her packages down carefully on the sidewalk beside her and laced and tied both shoes tightly.

"Can't lace 'em with a cane," said Phoenix. "Thank you, missy. I doesn't mind asking a nice lady to tie up my shoe when I gets out on the street."

Moving slowly and from side to side, she went into the stone building and into a tower of steps, where she walked up and around and around until her feet knew to stop.

70 She entered a door, and there she saw nailed up on the wall the document that had been stamped with the gold seal and framed in the gold frame which matched the dream that was hung up in her head.

"Here I be," she said. There was a fixed and ceremonial stiffness over her body.

"A charity case, I suppose," said an attendant who sat at the desk before her.

But Phoenix only looked above her head. There was sweat on her face; the wrinkles shone like a bright net.

"Speak up, Grandma" the woman said. "What's your name? We must have your history, you know. Have you been here before? What seems to be the trouble with you?"

75 Old Phoenix only gave a twitch to her face as if a fly were bothering her.

"Are you deaf?" cried the attendant.

But then the nurse came in.

"Oh, that's just old Aunt Phoenix," she said. "She doesn't come for herself—she has a little grandson. She makes these trips just as regular as clockwork. She lives away back off the Old Natchez Trace." She bent down. "Well, Aunt Phoenix, why don't you just take a seat? We won't keep you standing after your long trip." She pointed.

The old woman sat down, bolt upright in the chair.

"Now, how is the boy?" asked the nurse.

80 Old Phoenix did not speak.

"I said, how is the boy?"

But Phoenix only waited and stared straight ahead, her face very solemn and withdrawn into rigidity.

"Is his throat any better?" asked the nurse. "Aunt Phoenix, don't you hear me? Is your grandson's throat any better since the last time you came for the medicine?"

85   With her hand on her knees, the old woman waited, silent, erect,   85
and motionless, just as if she were in armor.

"You mustn't take up our time this way, Aunt Phoenix," the nurse said. "Tell us quickly about your grandson, and get it over. He isn't dead, is he?"

At last there came a flicker and then a flame of comprehension across her face, and she spoke.

"My grandson. It was my memory had left me. There I sat and forgot why I made my long trip."

"Forgot?" The nurse frowned. "After you came so far?"

90   Then Phoenix was like an old woman begging a dignified for-   90
giveness for waking up frightened in the night. "I never did go to school—I was too old at the Surrender," she said in a soft voice. "I'm an old woman without an education. It was my memory fail me. My little grandson, he is just the same, and I forgot it in the coming."

"Throat never heals, does it?" said the nurse, speaking in a loud, sure voice to Old Phoenix. By now she had a card with something written on it, a little list. "Yes, Swallowed lye. When was it—January—two—three years ago—"

Phoenix spoke unasked now. "No, missy, he not dead, he just the same. Every little while his throat begin to close up again, and he not able to swallow. He not get his breath. He not able to help himself. So the time come around, and I go on another trip for soothing medicine."

"All right. The doctor said as long as you came to get it you could have it," said the nurse. "But it's an obstinate case."

"My little grandson, he sit up there in the house all wrapped up, waiting by himself," Phoenix went on. "We is the only two left in the world. He suffer and it don't seem to put him back at all. He got a sweet look. He going to last. He wear a little patch quilt and peep out, holding his mouth open like a little bird. I remembers so plain now. I not going to forget him again, no, the whole enduring time. I could tell him from all the others in creation."

95 "All right." The nurse was trying to hush her now. She brought 95
her a bottle of medicine. "Charity," she said, making a check mark in
a book.

Old Phoenix held the bottle close to her eyes and then carefully
put it into her pocket.

"I thank you," she said.

"It's Christmas time, Grandma," said the attendant. "Could I give
you a few pennies out of my purse?"

"Five pennies is a nickel," said Phoenix stiffly.

100 "Here's a nickel," said the attendant. 100

Phoenix rose carefully and held out her hand. She received the
nickel and then fished the other nickel out of her pocket and laid it
beside the new one. She stared at her palm closely, with her head on
one side.

Then she gave a tap with her cane on the floor.

"This is what come to me to do," she said. "I going to the store
and buy my child a little windmill they sells, make out of paper. He
going to find it hard to believe there such a thing in the world. I'll
march myself back where he waiting, holding it straight up in this
hand."

She lifted her free hand, gave a little nod, turned round, and
walked out of the doctor's office. Then her slow step began on the
stairs, going down.

Newborn Thrown in Trash and Dies

John Edgar Wideman

John Edgar Wideman (1941–) spent a portion of his childhood years living in the Homewood section of Pittsburgh, a neighborhood that figures prominently in his fiction. He graduated from the University of Pennsylvania in 1963 and attended Oxford University on a Rhodes scholarship. Wideman has twice (1984 and 1991) received the prestigious PEN/Faulkner Award for his fiction. The most recent award was given for Philadelphia Fire *(1990), which* Publishers Weekly *called "a rich observation about the crumbling state of a once-beloved city." In 1992, Wideman published* The Short Stories of John Edgar Wideman, *and in 1994 the nonfiction work* Fatheralong: A Meditation on Fathers and Sons, Race and Society. *Wideman wrote the following short story after reading a newspaper account of a child who had been thrown down the garbage chute of an apartment building.*

1   They say you see your whole life pass in review the instant before you die. How would *they* know. If you die after the instant replay, you aren't around to tell anybody anything. So much for they and what they say. So much for the wish to be a movie star for once in your life because I think that's what people are hoping, what people are pretending when they say you see your life that way at the end. Death doesn't turn your life into a five-star production. The end is the end. And what you know at the end goes down the

"Newborn Thrown in Trash and Dies" by John Edgar Wideman, published in *All Stories Are True: The Stories of John Edgar Wideman*, Vintage Contemporaries, 1992.

tube with you. I can speak to you now only because I haven't reached the bottom yet. I'm on my way, faster than I want to be traveling and my journey won't take long, but I'm just beginning the countdown to zero. Zero's where I started also so I know a little bit about zero. Know what they say isn't necessarily so. In fact the opposite's true. You being and right in the eye of that instant storm your life plays itself out for you in advance. That's the theater of your fate, there's where you're granted a preview, the coming attractions of everything that must happen to you. Your life rolled into a ball so dense, so superheavy it would drag the universe down to hell if this tiny, tiny lump of whatever didn't dissipate as quickly as it formed. Quicker. The weight of what it is what you recall some infinitesimal fraction of when you stumble and crawl through your worst days on earth.

Knowledge of what's coming gone as quickly as it flashes forth. Quicker. Faster. Gone before it gets here, so to speak. Any other way and nobody would stick around to play out the cards they're dealt. No future in it. You being forgetting before the zero's entirely wiped off the clock face, before the next digit materializes. What they say is assbackwards, a saying by the way, assbackwards itself. Whether or not you're treated to a summary at the end, you get the whole thing handed to you, neatly packaged as you being. Then you forget it. Or try to forget. Live your life as if it hadn't happened before, as if the tape has not been prepunched full of holes, the die cast.

I remember because I won't receive much of a life. A measure of justice in the world, after all. I receive a compensatory bonus. Since the time between my wake-up call and curfew is so cruelly brief, the speeded-up preview of what will come to pass, my life, my portion, my destiny, my career, slowed down just enough to let me peek. Not slow enough for me to steal much, but I know some of what it contains, its finality, the groaning, fatal weight of it around my neck.

Call it a trade-off. A standoff. Intensity for duration. I won't get much and this devastating flash isn't much either, but I get it. Zingo.

But the future remains mysterious. Even if we all put our heads together and become one gigantic brain, a brain lots smarter than the sum of each of our smarts, an intelligence as great as the one that guides ants, whales or birds, because they're smarter, they figure things out not one by one, each individual locked in the cell of its head, its mortality, but collectively, doing what the group needs to do to survive, relate to the planet. If we were smarter even than birds and bees, we'd still have only a clue about what's inside the first flash of being. I know it happened and that I receive help from it. Scattered help. Sometimes I catch on. Sometimes I don't. But stuff from it's being pumped out always. I know things I have no business knowing. Things I haven't been around long enough to learn myself. For instance, many languages. A vast palette of feelings. The names of unseen things. Nostalgia for a darkness I've never experienced, a darkness another sense I can't account for assures me I will enter again. Large matters. Small ones. Naked as I am I'm dressed so to speak for my trip. Down these ten swift flight to oblivion.

Floor Ten. Nothing under the sun, they say, is new. This time they're right. They never stop talking so percentages guarantee they'll be correct sometimes. Especially since they speak out of both sides of their mouths at once: *Birds of a feather flock together. Opposites attract.* Like the billion billion monkeys at typewriters who sooner or later will bang out this story I think is uniquely mine. Somebody else, a Russian, I believe, with a long, strange-sounding name, has already written about his life speeding past as he topples slow-motion from a window high up in a tall apartment building. But it was another country. And alas, the Russian's dead.

Floor Nine. In this building they shoot craps. One of many forms of gambling proliferating here. Very little new wealth enters this cluster of buildings that are like high-rise covered wagons circled against the urban night, so what's here is cycled and recycled by games of chance, by murder and other violent forms of exchange. Kids do it. Adults. Birds and bees. The law here is the same one ruling the jungle, they say. They say this is a jungle of the urban asphalt concrete variety. Since I've never been to Africa or the Amazon I can't agree or disagree. But you know what I think about what they say.

Seven come eleven. Snake eyes. Boxcars. Fever in the funkhouse searching for a five. Talk to me, baby. Talk. Talk. Please. Please. Please

They cry and sing and curse and pray all night long over these games. On one knee they chant magic formulas to summon luck. They forget lock is rigged. Some of the men carry a game called Three Card Monte downtown. They cheat tourists who are stupid enough to trust in luck. Showmen with quick hands shuffling cards to a blur, fast feet carrying them away from busy intersections when cops come to break up their scam or hit on them for a cut. Flimflam artists, con men who daily use luck as bait and hook, down on their knees in a circle of other men who also should know better, trying to sweet-talk luck into their beds. Luck is the card you wish for, the card somebody else holds. You learn luck by its absence. Luck is what separates you from what you want. Luck is always turning its back and you lose.

10   Like other potions and powders they sell and consume here luck   10 creates dependency. In their rooms people sit and wait for a hit. A yearning unto death for more, more, more till the little life they've been allotted dies in a basket on the doorstep where they abandoned it.

The Floor of Facts. Seventeen stories in this building. The address is 2950 West 23rd Street. My mother is nineteen years old. The trash chute down which I was dropped is forty-five feet from the door of the apartment my mother was visiting. I was born and will die Monday, August 12, 1991. The small door in the yellow cinder block wall is maroon. I won't know till the last second why .my mother pushes it open. In 1990 nine discarded babies were discovered in New York City's garbage. As of August this year seven have been found. 911 is the number to call if you find a baby in the trash. Ernesto Mendez, forty-four, a Housing Authority caretaker, will notice my head, shoulders and curly hair in a black plastic bag he slashes open near the square entrance of the trash compactor on the ground floor of this brown-brick public housing project called the Gerald J. Carey Gardens. Gardens are green places where seeds are planted, tended, nurtured. The headline above my story reads "Newborn is Thrown in Trash and Dies." The headline will remind some readers of a similar story with a happy ending that appeared in March. A baby rescued and surviving after she was dropped down a trash chute by her twelve-year-old mother. The reporter, a Mr. George James who recorded many of the above facts, introduced my unhappy story in the Metro Section of the *New York Times* on Wednesday, August 14, with this paragraph: "A young Brooklyn woman gave birth on Monday afternoon in a stairwell in a Coney Island housing project and then dropped the infant down a trash chute into a compactor ten stories below, the police said yesterday." And that's about it. What's fit to print. My tale in a nutshell followed by a relation of facts obtained by interview and reading official documents. Trouble is I could not be reached for comment. No one's fault. Certainly no negligence on the reporter's part. He gave me sufficient notoriety. Many readers must have shaken their heads in dismay or sighed or blurted Jesus Christ, did you see this, handing the Metro Section across the breakfast table or passing it to somebody at work. As grateful as I am to have my story made public you should be able to understand why I feel cheated, why the newspaper account is not enough, why I want my voice to be part of the record. The awful silence is not truly broken until we speak for ourselves. One chance to speak was snatched away. Then I didn't cry out as I plunged through the darkness. I didn't know any better. Too busy thinking to myself, *This is how it is, this is how it is, how it is* … accustoming myself to what it seemed life brings, what life is. Spinning, tumbling, a breathless rush, terror, exhilaration and wonder, wondering is this it, am I doing it right. I didn't know any better. The floors, the other lives packed into this building were going on their merry way as I flew past them in the darkness of my tunnel. No one waved. No one warned me. Said hello or good-bye. And of course I was too busy flailing, trying to catch my breath, trying to stop shivering in the sudden, icy air, welcoming almost the thick, pungent draft rushing up at me as if another pair of thighs were opening below to replace the ones from which I'd been ripped.

In the quiet dark of my passage I did not cry out. Now I will not be still.

A Floor of Questions. Why.

A Floor of Questions. I believe the floor of fact should have been the ground floor, the foundation, the solid start, the place where all else is firmly rooted. I believe there should be room on the floor of fact for what I believe, for this opinion and others I could not venture before arriving here. I believe some facts sometimes speak for themselves but never speak for us. They are never anyone's voice and voices are what we must learn to listen to if we wish ever to be heard. I believe my mother did not hate me. I believe somewhere I have a father, who if he is reading this and listening carefully will recognize me as his daughter and be ashamed, heartbroken. I must believe these things. What else do I have. Who has made my acquaintance or noticed or cared or forgotten me. How could anyone be aware of what hurtles by faster than light, blankly, in a dark space beyond the walls of the rooms they live in, beyond the doors they lock, shades they draw when they have rooms and the rooms have windows and the windows have shades and the people believe they possess something worth concealing.

In my opinion my death will serve no purpose. The streetlamps will pop on. Someone will be run over by an expensive car in a narrow street and the driver will hear a bump but consider it of no consequence. Junkies will leak out the side doors of this gigantic mound, nodding, buzzing, greeting their kind with hipp-dip vocalizations full of despair and irony and stylized to embrace the very best that's being sung, played and said around them. A young woman will opened a dresser drawer and wonder whose baby that is sleeping peaceful on a bed of dishtowels, T-shirts, a man's ribbed sweat socks. She will feel something slither through the mud of her belly and splash into the sluggish river that meanders through her. She hasn't eaten for days, so that isn't it. Was it a deadly disease. Or worse, some new life she must account for. She opens and shuts the baby's drawer, pushes and pulls, opens and shuts.

I believe all floors are not equally interesting. Less reason to notice some than others. Equality would become boring, predictable. Though we may slight some and rattle on about others, that does not change the fact that each floor exists and the life on it is real, whether we pause to notice or not. As I gather speed and weight during my plunge, each floor adds its share. When I hit bottom I will bear witness to the truth of each one.

Floor of Wishes. I will miss Christmas. They say no one likes being born on Christmas. You lose your birthday, they say. A celebration already on December 25 and nice things happen to everyone on that day anyway, you give and receive presents, people greet you smiling and wish you peace and goodwill. The world is decorated. Colored bulbs draped twinkling in windows and trees, doorways hung with wild berries beneath which you may kiss a handsome stranger. Music everywhere. Even wars truced for twenty-four hours and troops served home-cooked meals, almost. Instead of at least two special days a year, if your birthday falls on Christmas, you lose one. Since my portion's less than a day, less than those insects called ephemera receive, born one morning, dead the next, and I can't squeeze a complete life cycle as they do into the time allotted, I wish today were Christmas. Once would be enough. If it's as special as they say. And in some matters we yearn to trust them. Need to trust something, someone, so we listen, wish what they say is true. The holiday of Christmas seems to be the best time on earth, to be a child and awaken with your eyes full of dreams and expectations and believe for a while at least that all good things are possible—peace, goodwill, love, merriment, the raven-maned rocking horse you want to ride forever. No conflict of interest for me. I wouldn't lose a birthday to Christmas. Rather than this smoggy heat I wish I could see snow. The city, this building snug under a blanket of fresh snow. No footprints of men running, men on their knees, men bleeding. No woman forced out into halls and streets, away from their children. I with this city, this tower were stranded in a gentle snowstorm and Christmas happens day after day and the bright fires in every hearth never go out, and the carols ring true chorus after chorus, and the gifts given and received precipitate endless joys. The world trapped in Christmas for a day dancing on forever. I wish I could transform the ten flights of my falling into those twelve days in the Christmas song. *On the first day of Christmas my true love said to me*...angels, a partridge in a pear tree, ten maids a milking, five gold rings, two turtledoves. I wish those would be the sights greeting me instead of darkness, the icy winter heart of the August afternoon I have been pitched without a kiss through a maroon door.

Floor of Power. El Presidente inhabits this floor. Some say he owns the whole building. He believes he owns it, collects rent, treats the building and its occupants with contempt. He is a bold-faced man. Cheeks slotted nose to chin like a puppet's. Chicken lips. This floor is entirely white. A floury, cracked white some say used to gleam. El Presidente is white also. Except for the pink dome of his forehead. Once, long ago, his flesh was pink head to toe. Then he painted himself white to match the white floor of power. Paint ran out just after the brush stroke that permanently sealed his eyes. Since El Presidente is cheap and mean he refused to order more paint. Since El Presidente is vain and arrogant he pretended to look at his unfinished self in the mirror and proclaimed he liked what he saw, the coat of cakey white, the raw, pink dome pulsing like a bruise.

El Presidente often performs on TV. We can watch him jog, golf, fish, travel, lie, preen, mutilate the language. But these activities are not his job; his job is keeping things in the building as they are, squatting on the floor of power like a broken generator or broken furnace of broken heart, occupying the space where one that works should be.

Floor of Regrets. One thing bothers me a lot. I regret not knowing what is on the floors above the one where I began my fall. I hope it's better up there. Real gardens perhaps or even a kind of heaven for the occupants lucky enough to live above the floors I've seen. Would one of you please mount the stairs, climb slowly up from floor ten, examine carefully, one soft, warm night, the topmost floors and sing me a lullaby of what I missed.

Floor of Love. I'm supposed to be sleeping. I could be sleeping. Early morning and my eyes don't want to open and legs don't want to push me out of bed yet. Two rooms away I can hear Mom in the kitchen. She's fixing breakfast. Daddy first, then I will slump into the kitchen Mom has made bright and smelling good already this morning. Her perkiness, the sizzling bacon, water boiling, wheat bread popping up like jack-in-the-box from the shiny toaster, the Rice Krispies crackling, fried eggs hissing, the FM's sophisticated patter and mincing string trios would wake the dead. And it does. Me and Daddy slide to our places. Hi, Mom. Good morning, Dearheart. The day begins. Smells wonderful. I awaken now to his hand under the covers with me, rubbing the baby fat of my tummy where he's shoved my nightgown up past my panties. He says I shouldn't wear them. Says it ain't healthy to sleep in your drawers. Says no wonder you get those rashes. He rubs and pinches. Little nips. Then the flat of this big hand under the elastic waistband wedges my underwear down. I raise my hips a little bit to help. No reason not to. The whole thing be over with sooner. Don't do no good to try and stop him or slow him down. He said my Mama knows. He said go on fool and tell her she'll smack you for talking nasty. He was right. She beat me in the kitchen. Then took me in to their room and he stripped me butt-naked and beat me again while she watched. So I kinda hump up, wiggle, and my underwear's down below my knees, his hand's on its way back up to where I don't even understand how to grow hairs yet.

The Floor That Stands for All the Other Floors Missed or Still to Come. My stepbrother Tommy was playing the schoolyard and they shot him dead. Bang. Bang. Gang banging and poor Tommy caught a cap in his chest. People been in and out of the apartment all day. Sorry. Sorry. Everybody's so sorry. Some brought cakes, pies, macaroni casseroles, lunch meat, liquor. Two Ebony Cobras laid a joint on Tommy's older brother who hadn't risen from the kitchen chair he's straddling, head down, nodding, till his boys bop through the door. They know who hit Tommy. They know tomorrow what they must do. Today one of those everybody-in-the-family-and-friends-in-dark-clothes-funeral days, the mothers, sisters, aunts, grandmothers weepy, the men motherfucking everybody from god on down. You can't see me among the mourners. My time is different from this time. You can't understand my time. Or name it. Or share it. Tommy is beginning to remember me. To join me where I am falling unseen through your veins and arteries down to where the heart stops, the square opening through which trash passes to the compactor.

The Red Wheelbarrow

William Carlos Williams

William Carlos Williams (1883–1963) was born in Rutherford, New Jersey. He wrote poetry, fiction, nonfiction, and plays there while simultaneously working as a pediatrician. He published his first book, Poems, *in 1909, and was posthumously awarded the Pulitzer Prize for poetry in 1963 for* Pictures from Brueghel *(1962). The following selection, written in the early 1920s, reflects Williams' desire to write poetry in speech-like language uncomplicated by abstract concepts.*

so much depends
upon

a red wheel
barrow

glazed with rain
water

beside the white
chickens.

"The Red Wheelbarrow" by William Carlos Williams, published in *The Collected Poems of William Carlos Williams, Volume I, 1909–1939*, Edited by Christopher MacGowan, Copyright 1938, 1944, 1945 by William Carlos Williams. New Directions Publishing Group.

The Second Coming

William Butler Yeats

William Butler Yeats (1865-1939), though born in Dublin, spent his early years in London. His father was the painter John Butler Yeats; his mother's family was from County Sligo in Ireland. Yeats began as a painter but quickly turned to poetry and drama. His fascination with pagan Irish mythology and the occult led him to produce works that reflected Irish legends and other mysterious stories and beings. He founded the Irish National Theatre in 1899. After the Irish rebellion of 1916, he became an avid nationalist and served as a senator from 1922 through 1928. In 1923 he received the Nobel Prize for literature. His first book of poems was The Wanderings of Oisin and Other Poems *(1889) and his first play* The Countess Cathleen *(1892). Later works include* The Green Helmet and Other Poems *(1910),* Michael Robartes and the Dancer *(1921), the autobiographical* A Vision *(1925), and* The Tower *(1928). "The Second Coming" contains many of Yeats' most important symbols and images compacted into a powerful twenty-two lines.*

1   Turning and turning in the widening gyre   1
The falcon cannot hear the falconer;
Things fall apart; the center cannot hold;
Mere anarchy is loosed upon the world,
5   The blood-dimmed tide is loosed, and everywhere   5
The ceremony of innocence is drowned;
The best lack all conviction, while the worst
Are full of passionate intensity.

Surely some revelation is at hand;
Surely the Second Coming is at hand.
The Second Coming! Hardly are those words out
When a vast image out of *Spiritus Mundi*
Troubles my sight: somewhere in sands of the desert
A shape with lion body and the head of a man,
A gaze blank and pitiless as the sun,
Is moving its slow thighs, while all about it
Reel shadows of the indignant desert birds.
The darkness drops again; but now I know
That twenty centuries of stony sleep
Were vexed to nightmare by a rocking cradle,
And what rough beast, its hour come round at last,
Slouches toward Bethlehem to be born?

"The Song of Wandering Aengus"
William B. Yeats

William Butler Yeats (1865–1939), though born in Dublin, spent his early years in London. His father was the painter John Bulter Yeats; his mother's family was from County Silgo in Ireland. Yeats began as a painter but quickly turned to poetry and drama. His facisnation with pagan Irish mythology and the occult led him to produce works that reflected Irish legends and other mysterious stories and beings. He founded the Irish National Theatre in 1899. After the Irish rebellion of 1916, he became an avid nationalist and served as a senator from 1922 through 1928. In 1923 he received the Nobel Prize for literature. His first book of poems was The Wanderings of Oisin and Other Poems *(1889) and his first play* The Countess Cathleen *(1892). Later works include* The Green Helmet and Other Poems *(1910),* Michael Robartes and the Dancer *(1921), the autobiographical* A Vision *(1925), and the* Tower *(1928). In "The Song of Wandering Aengus" Yeats asks what a person learns from spititual encounters: does one come away with new knowledge or is one simply overcome by awe?*

1 I went out to the hazel wood,   1
  Because a fire was in my head,
  And cut and peeled a hazel wand,
  And hooked a berry to a thread;
5 And when white moths were on the wing, 5

And moth-like stars were flickering out,
I dropped the berry in a stream
And caught a little silver trout.

When I had laid it on the floor
I went to blow the fire aflame,
But something rustled on the floor,
And some one called me by my name:
It had become a glimmering girl
With apple blossom in her hair
Who called me by my name and ran
And faded through the brightening air.

Though I am old with wandering
Through hollow lands and hilly lands,
I will find out where she has gone,
And kiss her lips and take her hands;
And walk among long dappled grass,
And pluck till time and times are done
The silver apples of the moon,
The golden apples of the sun.